MATTHEW
ARNOLD

~~ MATTHEW ARNOLD ~~
(From the portrait by Watts)
"He took dejectedly
His seat upon the Intellectual Throne"

MATTHEW ARNOLD

By HUGH KINGSMILL

LINCOLN MAC VEAGH

THE DIAL PRESS · NEW YORK

LONGMANS, GREEN & COMPANY
TORONTO
1928

PRINTED IN THE UNITED STATES OF AMERICA
BY THE VAIL-BALLOU PRESS, INC., BINGHAMTON, N. Y.

CONTENTS

v

LIST OF ILLUSTRATIONS

Ah, love, let us be true
To one another! for the world, which seems
To lie before us like a land of dreams,
So various, so beautiful, so new,
Hath really neither joy, nor love, nor light,
Nor certitude, nor peace, nor help for pain;
And we are here as on a darkling plain
Swept with confused alarms of struggle and flight,
Where ignorant armies clash by night.

Matthew Arnold

Jesus hits the plain natural truth that human life
is a blessing and a benefit. . . .

Matthew Arnold

INTRODUCTION

ONE evening in the late autumn of 1912 Middleton Murry called on Frank Harris, at the offices of *Hearth and Home,* a mild ladies' paper, which, after a long and blameless life, suddenly found itself struggling in the fierce embraces of Frank Harris, endured during six months the extremes of ecstasy and remorse, and died in the following year. In the spring of 1912 Murry, then twenty-two or three, had written of Harris as the biggest man since Shakespeare. Harris was content enough with this as a provisional estimate, but was waiting for it to be amplified.

As Murry entered the room on this evening, Harris, who had been brooding over ladies' underwear at the editorial desk, swivelled round and fixed his disciple with a firm eye.

"Well," he boomed, "and what are you writing now?" Murry, with strange imprudence, but he was very young, replied that he was thinking of writing a study of Matthew Arnold.

"Matthew Arnold!" Harris glared across at me, and I blushed. Murry suddenly looked very old. "Matthew Arnold! You might as well write. . . ." The door opened to admit a nervous gentlewoman who did the fashions above the pen-name of Lady Betty. Harris turned to her and flung out his hands with a roar— "He might as well write on——"

The image employed by Harris must have come between Murry and the sheet of paper whenever he sat down to begin for he has not yet given us this study. Should he read the following pages, he may perhaps be stimulated to address himself yet once again to the task. The view of Arnold taken in this book would seem to him, if not at all points unsound, yet in great need of correction.

Since the French Revolution many poets, in prose or verse, have left their proper work and become prophets; Coleridge, for example, and Tolstoi, Nietzsche, Carlyle, Ruskin and Arnold himself; and more recently H. G. Wells, Belloc and Chesterton. One might add Bernard Shaw, if the German or Elizabethan use of the word poet could be stretched to include him.

The theme of this book is the collapse of a poet into a prophet. Such a theme requires personal treatment; and I have had to keep Arnold, chiefly with the help of his poems and letters, continuously before the reader's eyes. Nothing, I admit with compunction, would have disconcerted him more. He was always insisting that the critic's business is to get himself completely out of the way, to lay the actual facts before the reader, and leave it to the reader to form his own conclusions. This sounds modest, until we ask on what grounds Arnold assumes himself to be in possession of the actual facts. It then becomes clear that Arnold's desire to vanish into a cavern, from which his voice will presently emerge with the authority of something abstract and impersonal, is due not to modesty but to prudence. The omniscient like a certain distance between themselves and their audience.

This distance I have annihilated, leading Arnold out of the wings and placing him boldly upstage. In this situation he may lose in impressiveness, but he will gain in human interest.

The inferences about his private life, drawn from his poems and other sources, are not, I believe, pushed too far. There is something about a Puritan poet, and especially about a Victorian Puritan poet, that imposes a certain caution and deference on even the most exuberant believer in biographical frankness. A few years ago Dr. Harper exposed the fact that Wordsworth in his youth had had a love-affair with a French girl, who had borne him a child and whom he had then deserted. In most of the comments I read on this incident the critics wrote as if Wordsworth had magnanimously suspended his celibacy as part of a general programme for the renovation of humanity; or had at worst committed a slight error of judgment in his anxiety to get into line with the finer spirits of the French Revolution.

As I have used Arnold's personal history to explain his weaknesses as a poet and a critic, I should, logically, supply the reader with a memoir of myself, to enable him without trouble to locate the gaps in my own knowledge and experience. Every biography ought to be preceded by a sketch of the writer's own life. If the reader learnt from this sketch that the biographer was happily married, he would be able to gauge fairly accurately how far that mixed state of resignation and dubious self-approval had influenced the biographer's view of Wagner's private life, or Casanova's, or Shelley's. Conversely, if the biographer's intimate affairs were in some confusion, the reader would understand the alternation of annoyance and patronage in a picture of Tennyson's monogamous felicity.

Also, the tendency of biographers to be omniscient would be corrected by such a sketch. The biographer would be required to state his knowledge of foreign languages, and the sciences; his experience, if any, of business and war; the countries he had visited, and the duration of his stay in each; and his social status, at birth and present day.

It would be well for such sketches to be passed as accurate by a board of three rival biographers.

An unknown writer cannot venture on such an innovation, but perhaps some famous author of the day will read this preface, and be tempted to make the experiment. Mr. H. G. Wells, for example, with his hatred of the petty egotism of the individual, might give us an account of the leper priest, Father Damien, with parallel instances of self-abnegation in his own life.

As a partial solution of this autobiography problem I have written this study as informally as possible, avoiding the exhaustive treatment in which the personal relation of the critic to his subject is submerged in an impersonal and omniscient examination of all the subject's activities. I am not competent to discuss Arnold's writings on education, and have therefore left them alone, nor have I dealt with his prose in detail, but only so far as it illustrates the disintegration of the poet into the prophet, the sole theme of this book.

I. SANCTITY OF PRIVATE LIFE UNDER QUEEN
VICTORIA

I T is at present unfashionable to attack the Victorians.
I infer this from the number of articles I have read
in the last year or so, in which the writers have represented themselves as immune from the present fashion
of attacking the Victorians.

The credit of the Victorian age was at its lowest in
the decade before the war, a phase which was ended by
Lytton Strachey's "Eminent Victorians." It was impossible for anyone to be more amusing at the expense
of the Victorians than Lytton Strachey had been; some
other attitude was therefore necessary. Strachey himself felt that necessity. There is a perceptible change of
tone in his "Queen Victoria," which was published, I
think, in 1921, three years after "Eminent Victorians."
But Strachey was too individual to be stampeded from
one extreme to the other. Michael Sadleir, the biographer of Anthony Trollope, is a better example of the
reaction towards Victorianism. Here is a quotation from
him which I came across the other day: "Those of an
older generation than my own have, perhaps, never
betrayed their gentile Victorian heritage. One may envy
and applaud their wisdom. But we prodigals, returned
from our rioting and sick with the husks of a *démodé*
violence, stoop to any self-abasement, to any denial of

6

our own past judgment, so we be allowed entry to the quiet courts and ordered opulence of the age we once affected to despise."

I remember Sadleir in 1812 when he was assisting Middleton Murry, in the pages of "Rhythm," to herd the swine in fashion at that epoch; and very fine beasts some of them were, too. A faint friendliness has existed between us since that date, and I should not care to dissipate it by a sharp word. I shall therefore maintain a humane reticence about this quotation, which I have given only in order to show that any unfavourable comments I make on the Victorian age are not due to a belief that I am conforming with the fashion of the moment.

Now for a few unfavourable comments. George Russell writes as follows in his introduction to Arnold's letters, which were brought out in 1895: "It was Matthew Arnold's express wish that he might not be made the subject of a Biography. His family, however, felt that a selection from his letters was not prohibited; and that such a selection might reveal aspects of his character, his tenderness and playfulness and filial affection—which could be only imperfectly apprehended through the more formal medium of his published works. . . . Here and there I have been constrained, by deference to living susceptibilities, to make some slight excisions; but, as regards the bulk of the Letters, this process had been performed before the manuscript came into my hands."

The Victorians either, like Thackeray and Carlyle

and Arnold, expressly desired that their biographies should not be written, or, like Tennyson and Dickens, got a son or a dependable friend to do the job. It would be incorrect to infer from this that the Victorians were given over, in their private lives, to the practice of cannibalism, black magic, incest, etc.; and no such inference, as a matter of fact, has as yet been drawn from their frantic anxiety to muffle their personal affairs in obscurity. I should say that as late as 1910 the writers I have just mentioned were popularly regarded as completely respectable and, except Arnold, orthodox. Carlyle, certainly, had been damaged by Froude, but not in his respectability. Froude painted him as a harsh and selfish husband, but no sexual irregularities were suggested. On the contrary, Froude implied that it would be stretching the facts to call Carlyle as much as a monogamist. Even Dickens' separation from his wife was not regarded with mistrust. Dickens, it was explained, was of a highly nervous temperament; also, his heart was in the grave of his wife's youngest sister. As late as the middle of King Edward's reign, G. K. Chesterton had a rhetorical spasm over the tearing apart of two decent God-fearing persons as though "by a blast of bigamy or adultery."

Since the war the legend that the great men of the Victorian age differed essentially from the great men of all other ages is beginning to crack; and it is generally becoming accepted, in spite of the present opposing current of sentimentalism, that there is nothing indecorous in assuming Dickens, Thackeray, Browning and the other Victorians to have been as subject to human weaknesses as Goethe, Balzac and Tolstoi.

That it should ever have been indecorous to make such an assumption is a sign of the extraordinary mental distortion induced by Victorian respectability. In a book recently published, called "Mainly Victorian," the author, S. M. Ellis,[1] bursts into the following apostrophe:

"Blessed period of peace and prosperity, port and progeny and domesticity *in excelsis* from Buckingham Palace to Bloomsbury Square and brand-new Bayswater. Despite its limitations, it was a good, solid, happy time of English life at its best."

That is the effect made by Victorian respectability on what S. M. Ellis would undoubtedly call this age of cocktails and concupiscence and domesticity *in profundis;* but it is an illusion.

In 1725, when Clive was a small boy, his Uncle Bayley wrote about him in these terms: "I am satisfied his fighting (to which he is out of measure addicted) gives his temper a fierceness and imperiousness that he flies out upon every trifling occasion, for this reason I do what I can to suppress the heroic that I may help forward the more valuable qualities of Meekness, Benevolence and Patience."

This quotation has a Victorian ring. It would be

---

[1] Mr. Ellis wrote a very interesting life of Meredith, in which he disclosed the obscene fact that Meredith's father was a tailor. The book had to be withdrawn from publication, nominally because Mr. Ellis had infringed someone's copyright. Mr. Ellis' enthusiasm over the Victorian spirit is creditable to his temper.

difficult to sum up the Victorian ideal more succinctly than in Uncle Bayley's "I do what I can to suppress the Heroic." But Uncle Bayley is solid. He has no qualms; no secret disquiet when contemplating the qualities of Meekness, Benevolence and Patience. Living in the dawn of England's industrial age, he regards the Heroic with placid bovine disapproval. Set this massive creature by the side of any Victorian, and how divided, uncertain and tormented the latter shows! He is much richer than Uncle Bayley, and the pile of his money-bags is increasing. But between him and Uncle Bayley's dawn is the bloody noon of the French Revolution, and now in the thickening twilight he discerns hideous shapes stealing towards him—Disbelief, rampant, and Social Unrest, and Lubricity, a wanton from France; and it occurs to him, for the hundredth time, that the two sentries mounted over his money-bags, Sanctity-of-the-Home and Belief-in-a-Future-Life, look as if they were beginning to sicken for something.

If this is a true image of Victorianism, the value set by Victorian writers on their respectibility is seen to be the value naturally set by a man on his stock-in-trade. Some of them, it is true, were always a little uncertain in their attempts to gratify the popular frenzy for Purity, Family Life, etc. That Thackeray, for example, hadn't his heart in the business was felt by many of his readers. Yet, Heaven knows, the poor man did his best to correct this impression. Having set out in Pendennis to paint a Man, in the bold fashion of Fielding, he brings Arthur Pendennis, after an idle and extravagant life at the Varsity, up to London. The scene, to a reader of Fielding, would appear to be set for a little debauchery. But Arthur has a mother, and mothers, though relatively even more numerous than to-day, were sacred in the Victorian age; and Arthur's mother has an adopted daughter, Laura, whom Arthur regards as a sister, until he marries her in the last chapter. Sisters, allowing for age, were as sacred to the Victorians as mothers. It follows, therefore, by the processes of Victorian logic, that the sacredness of these two women compels Arthur to regard all women as sacred. He continues to be idle and extravagant, he has his moments of scepticism (on matters unconnected with sex or religion), but he retains his chastity.

Yet there were many who still charged Thackeray with cynicism.

After a rest-cure from his age in "Esmond" (the hero of which book regards the heroine as a mother until he marries her in the last chapter), Thackeray set to again and wrote the "Newcomes," which opens with Colonel Newcome and his son Clive visiting a Victorian night-club, for men only, the Cave of Harmony. An indelicate song is sung, and the Colonel marches his son out, after laying his stick across the shoulders of every man in the room.

This incident provoked no surprise in the Victorian reader, many of whom were now converted from their previous view that Thackeray was cynical.

He again retired to the Eighteen Century, but with a better heart this time, bearing with him a Victorian youth, Harry Warrington, a boon companion of George Selwyn and the other rakes of that age, yet, Thackeray insists, "wild not wicked"; though he does not tell us in what terms Harry begged to be excused from the company when the fun became fast as well as furious.

After this very few persons called Thackeray a cynic, and those who did were probably above rather than below the general level of intelligence.

But Thackeray lacked a natural relish for the job; one of the reasons perhaps which led to his famous quarrel with Dickens, whose innocent fun when he was marrying off the young women at the close of his novels must have maddened Thackeray with the contrast between his own forced tricklings and this gushing forth as from some inexhaustible spring of natural imbecility. Nor did Dickens command only in the realm of legalized endearments. He possessed, though he exercised it only at discreet intervals, an equal command in the outer region where flitted the outcasts whose endearments were unlegalized. His "unfortunates" emerge suddenly out of the night to gaze with hungry despair at the face of a Rose Maylie or a Little Dorrit . . . they, too, once . . . oh, Heavens! . . . then back into the pitchy blackness with a wild unearthly cry; leaving the modern reader to wonder at the nerves of tempered steel the Victorian *roué* must have possessed to get into bed against odds like these.

In calling a prostitute an "unfortunate" the Victorians wished to imply that a prostitute was someone who had invested in the wrong stock, in spite of the advice of more experienced investors.

Hence the questions which Hood asks about the prostitute who commits suicide in his poem, "The Bridge of Sighs":

> "Who was her father?
> Who was her mother?
> Had she a sister?
> Had she a brother?"

These questions are not asked for the sake of information. They are purely rhetorical. Hood knew well that his heroine was one of a large and otherwise innocent family, and had come into lack of existence simply to illustrate what happens to a girl who neglects the practical counsel of her relatives. Such counsels had been given her freely, but she had ignored them, and therefore

> "Sisterly, brotherly,
> Fatherly, motherly
> Feelings had changed."

It is as a blackleg against the trade union of the Family that Hood sees her. She is "rash and undutiful," she has been guilty of "mutiny"; and that is the final impression of the poem in spite of signs here and there that Hood sees her also as an individual, related to the tragedy of life directly and not as a unit of the family system.

"Mutiny" of a far grosser kind, because committed against a husband, is also the keynote of Arthur's farewell address to Guinevere, a Victorian document of unequalled importance. Its extreme popularity with the Victorians as a moving and magnanimous expression of the correct attitude towards an unfaithful wife entitles it to a lengthy analysis. Besides, in a brief summary, I might be suspected of caricaturing it. The poem opens as follows:

> "Queen Guinevere had fled the court, and sat
> There in the holy house at Almesbury,
> Weeping, none with her save a little maid,
> A novice."

She has parted for the last time from her lover, Lancelot, whose adultery with her has disintegrated the morale of Arthur's court, and as a result encouraged an attack from "the godless Hosts of heathen swarming o'er the Northern Sea."

The task assigned by Tennyson to the little maid is to break what is left of Guinevere's spirit before Arthur arrives.

The novice begins with a depressing little ditty:

> "No light! so late! and dark and chill the night!
> O let us in that we may find the light!
> Too late, too late: ye cannot enter now."

The Queen weeps, and the novice, who sees in her only a noble stranger, consoles her. She cannot be sorrowing, the novice says, for evil done—"right sure am I of that"—and, whatever her sorrow, it will seem less if she weighs it against "our Lord the King's," who has gone

> "To wage grim war against Sir Lancelot there,
>   Round that strong castle where he holds the Queen,"

and so on for another eighteen lines.

The Queen agrees with the novice about the sympathy due to Arthur, and the novice begins again:

> "This is all woman's grief
>   That *she* is woman, whose disloyal life
>   Hath wrought confusion in the Table Round. . . ."

The Queen tries to dam the novice's flow, but in vain. It so happened that the little maid's father had been a knight of the Round Table; and he had often told her of the signs and wonders that filled the land when the Table was founded, and of the universal gladness before the coming of "the sinful Queen." There was, too, a bard who had prophesied that if Arthur could find "a woman in her womanhood as great as he was in his manhood . . ." etc., etc.

Guinevere tries yet again to close the topic, only to give occasion for another contrast between herself and "the sinful Queen."

At last she breaks down and orders the novice out of the room. Tennyson allows himself and the Queen a breathing-space. Then:

> "On a sudden a cry: 'The King.' She sat
>   Stiff—stricken, listening; but when armed feet

Thro' the long gallery from the open doors
Rang coming, prone from off her seat she fell
And grovell'd with her face against the floor."

Arthur enters, and at once opens out into an enormous
speech, to which Guinevere listens throughout with her
face on the floor, shifting her position only once, in
order to clasp her husband's feet.

The main divisions of this address, which is a most
careful piece of work, and was probably committed to
memory before it was delivered, are as follows:

1. A general indictment of Guinevere on the ground
that she had ruined his life's work.

"Well is it that no child is born of thee.
The children born of thee are sword and fire,
Red ruin and the breaking-up of laws. . . ."

2. A frank appraisement of his life's work.

"I was first of all the kings who drew
The knighthood-errant of this realm and all
The realms together under me, their Head,
In that fair Order of the Table Round,
A glorious company. . . ."

3. Death the only cure.

"How sad it were for Arthur should he live
To sit once more within his lonely hall. . . ."

4. Love versus duty to the public.

"For think not, tho' thou wouldst not love thy lord,
Thy lord has wholly lost his love for thee.

I am not made of so slight elements.
Yet must I leave thee, woman, to thy shame.
I hold that man the worst of public foes
Who either for his own or children's sake,
To save his blood from scandal, lets the wife
Whom he knows false, abide and rule the house."

5. Portrait of a wife who has been reinstated after a single infidelity.

"She, like a new disease, unknown to men,
Creeps, no precaution used, among the crowd,
Makes wicked lightnings of her eyes, and saps
The fealty of his friends and stirs the pulse
With devil's leaps, and poisons half the young."

6. Change of key, to correct a possible misapprehension that his previous remarks carried an unfriendly sense.

"I did not come to curse thee, Guinevere,
I whose vast pity almost makes me die. . . ."

7. Forgiveness—His and God's.

"Lo! I forgive thee, as eternal God
Forgives."

8. Remarriage in Heaven, after she has been to the cleaners.

"Perchance, and so thou purify thy soul,
And so thou lean on our fair father Christ,
Hereafter in that world where all are pure,
We two may meet before high God, and thou

Wilt spring to me, and claim me thine, and know
I am thine husband—not a smaller soul,
Nor Lancelot, nor another."

I have now set forth, fairly completely, the ideal world towards which the Victorians strained. It was not, of course, the actual Victorian world. Even under Victoria the nights were not shrill with the inhuman cries of domestic blacklegs, and a company of men ran no risk of being thrashed in rotation if they listened to a bawdy song without first making sure that no one present had brought a father with him. The female members of a family did not cast anti-aphrodisiacal spells over their absent menfolk, nor did a wife who had preferred another man to her husband glue her face to the floor, while the husband explained how impossible it was to admit a harlot like her into decent society.

These things did not occur, but it gratified the Victorians to believe they did. In such an atmosphere Casanova himself would have become reticent, and Benevenuto Cellini vague; while for any reasonably respectable person the fear that he might fall into the hands of a truthful biographer must have become, and indeed obviously did become, a continuous nightmare.

II. IN DEFERENCE TO LIVING SUSCEPTIBILITIES

HAVING placed Matthew Arnold's express wish that he might not be made the subject of a Biography in its proper perspective, I can now return to George Russell's Introduction to Arnold's Letters.

"Here and there," Mr. Russell writes, in the passage I have quoted, "I have been constrained, by deference to living susceptibilities, to make some slight excisions; but, as regards the bulk of the Letters, this process had been performed before the manuscript came into my hands."

Swinburne was alive when George Russell published these Letters. He had been the first, in a long and enthusiastic essay written in the 'sixties, to draw general attention to Arnold's poetry; and Arnold himself had acknowledged the good Swinburne had done him by this appreciation.

There are five references to Swinburne in these letters, and they are all unflattering. George Russell's "deference to living susceptibilities" did not operate where someone out of sympathy with the Victorian attitude was concerned.

I give these references, because their inclusion in two volumes otherwise almost entirely freed from personalities is a typical by-product of Victorian morality.

In 1863, Arnold wrote to his mother that he had been dining with Monckton Milnes, where he had met "a sort of pseudo-Shelley called Swinburne."

In 1865, he wrote to J. Conington: "Swinburne's poem is, as you say," it being plain from the context that J. Conington had not said anything agreeable.

In 1867, after Swinburne had praised Arnold, Arnold wrote to his mother. . . . "I am to meet Swinburne at dinner on Monday . . . he expresses a great desire to meet me, and I should like to do him some good, but I am afraid he has taken some bent."

In 1870, in a letter to his mother, he gave as one of the discouraging signs of the times the fact that Swinburne was "the favourite poet of the young men at Oxford." And in 1882 he wrote to Sir Mountstuart Grant Duff that Swinburne had sent him his "Tristram of Lyonesse" "with a pretty letter . . . his fatal habit of using one hundred words where one would suffice always offends me."

Swinburne, of course, saw these references, and a doubtless faint echo of his resentment sounds in one of his last essays, where he speaks of Matthew Arnold as "a man whose main achievement in creative literature was to make himself by painful painstaking into a sort of pseudo-Wordsworth."

I remember George Russell in the School Chapel at Harrow. He was always emotional over Harrow, his old school, and used frequently to come down from London to the Sunday evening service.

Like Tennyson's Arthur, he was tall and stout, with a white, flaccid face, but unlike Arthur did not carry a beard.

III. DR. ARNOLD AS NULLUS

MATTHEW ARNOLD was born in 1822, and was married in 1851. About this period, far the most important in his life, there is, for reasons already sufficiently explained, hardly any direct information. Something, however, can be gathered by inference, from his poems and other sources. Inference, therefore, will be unsparingly used.

I used to think Matt must have regarded his father with strongly qualified admiration. But a closer study of Matt's letters shows that such revulsion against his father's view of life as he certainly felt for a year or two in his youth was succeeded by a renewed surrender, permanent this time though never quite complete, to his father's personality.

Until Lytton Strachey published his study of Dr. Arnold in "Eminent Victorians," the popular impression of Arnold was taken from Thomas Hughes' picture of him in "Tom Brown's School-days," a school story which appeared in the 'fifties, the fatal decade of "The Newcomes" and "The Idylls of the King." Although the nature of the book excluded any direct feminine interest, the extreme importance attached at that time to the purifying influence of a good woman so mesmerized Thomas Hughes that by the close of the story the fragile and spiritual Arthur is transformed into the stock Victorian heroine. I haven't the book by me, but I can remember how Arthur nearly dies, and how Tom Brown visits him in bed, and takes his white, slender hand, on which the blue veins stand out pathetically, in his own brown freckled paw, and is filled with remorse for his irregular past and with aspirations towards a purer future. All one misses is the nurse laying the new-born child in the father's arms.

Dr. Arnold, himself, seen through this atmosphere, lacks actuality. He is immensely stern in public, and immensely tender and understanding in private. A brooding love for his young charges is suggested throughout, and an entire absorption in the glorious task of forming youthful character. Dr. Arnold's real feeling about boys and public schools and his own relation to Rubgy and the world in general was not at all what Thomas Hughes imagined.

The only authority on Dr. Arnold of any importance is the Life of him by Dean Stanley, one of his favourite pupils, from whom, however, Arnold decidedly withheld the secrets of literary composition.

None the less, the book contains enough material to enable its readers, if any, to piece together a fairly clear view of its subject.

Shortly after leaving Oxford Arnold wrote to one of his friends: "I believe that naturally I am one of the most ambitious men alive," and he goes on to give the three chief objects of human ambition "to be the Prime Minister of a great kingdom, the governor of a great

DR. ARNOLD
(The famous Rugby Headmaster)
He wanted to be Cæsar or nothing

empire, or the writer of works which should live in every age and in every country." At that time he was earning his living as tutor to private pupils, at Laleham in the Thames valley, an unambitious form of existence on which he comments to another friend. "I have always thought that I should like to be *aut Cæsar aut nullus*, and as it is pretty well settled for me that I shall not be *Cæsar*, I am quite content to live in peace as *nullus*."

He was further reconciled to his obscurity by his fear of becoming worldly. The religious element in his nature discountenanced all ambition: such at least would seem to be the meaning of this sentence of Dean Stanley's: "He was not insensible to the attractions of visions of extensive influence, and almost to his latest hour he seems to have been conscious of the existence of the temptation within him, and of the necessity of contending against it."

But as the years passed we find him modifying the crude formula *aut Cæsar aut nullus*, until the disharmony between ambition and religion almost vanishes.

"I cannot tell you," he writes to a friend, "how the present state of the country occupies my mind and what a restless desire I feel that it were in my power to do any good." "What say you," he writes to Dr. Whateley, "to a work on πολιτικὴ in the old Greek sense of the word, in which I should try to apply the principles of the Gospel to the legislation and administration of a state? It would begin with a simple statement of the Τέλος of man according to Christianity." He is troubled, too, by the extreme felicity of his home life at Laleham, confessing a "fear that this earthly happiness may interest me too much."

So, in one way and another, he finds respectable reasons for being no longer content with the state of a *nullus*, though there can be no question that the earthly happiness he speaks of was genuinely felt by him during his eight years at Laleham. He enjoyed his work, and was on affectionate and even playful terms with his pupils, gambolling with them during recreational hours in a fashion rather hard to visualize at this distance, and through the medium of Dean Stanley's prose. He was playful with his family, too, and profoundly tender. Dean Stanley speaks of "the rare, the unbroken, the almost awful happiness of his domestic life."

The friends he had made at Oxford were another source of happiness. He would write to them at length on politics, religion, and his favourite Greek and Roman writers. His formal style warms and quickens at the touch of the classics. "Now for your remarks about my Poppo," he writes breathlessly to one friend, and to another he croons over "dear old Tottle's Politics." Modern literature he seems not to have cared for, and Byron, to whom there are two or three references, he disliked. " 'Don Juan' has been with me for some weeks, but I am determined not to read it, for I was so annoyed by some specimens that I saw in glancing over the leaves, that I will not worry myself with any more of it."

It is hard to imagine Dr. Arnold not occupied in some way, but in one letter, written shortly after he went to Laleham, he relieves us for a moment from the barren spectacle of continuous activity. "Laleham is very beautiful, and some of the scenes at the junction of the heath country with the rich valley of the Thames are very striking. . . . I have always a resource at hand in the bank of the river up to Staines; which, though it be perfectly flat, has yet a great charm from its entire loneliness, there being not a house anywhere near it; the river here has none of that stir of boats and barges upon it, which makes it in many places as public as the high road"; and with this we may connect a desire he expressed towards the close of his life that his "bones should go to Grasmere churchyard, to lie under the yews which Wordsworth planted, and to have the Rotha with its deep and silent pools passing by."

ARNOLD was only thirty-one when he applied for and obtained the headmastership of Rugby. His application arrived late, and he himself was unknown to the board of selection. The board, however, had received a letter from Dr. Hawkins, later Provost of Oriel, in which Dr. Hawkins predicted that Arnold, if appointed headmaster of Rugby, would change the face of education all through the public schools of England; and this letter decided them in Arnold's favour.

"My view of things certainly becomes daily more reforming," Arnold wrote, after his election. "My object will be, if possible, to form Christian men, for Christian boys I can scarcely hope to make." That was the view of boys he took at the beginning of his headmastership, and experience confirmed and deepened it.

He would not even have understood, far less approved, the Victorian cult of Boys for boys' sake, begun in "Tom Brown's School-days," and finding varied forms in "Eric," the poems of the Etonian master, Cory, and Bowen's Harrow songs, down to the novels of E. F. Benson and other connoisseurs in the charm, naturalness, animal grace, etc., of the adolescent male.

At the beginning of his headmastership, Arnold speaks of "the natural imperfect state of boyhood."

Towards the close, he is filled with a sense of "evil of boy-nature, which makes me always unwilling to undergo the responsibility of advising anyone to send his son to a public school."

To exorcise, as far as possible, this evil, was the sole aim of his headmastership, and the instruments with which he worked where the older boys, whom he laboured unintermittently to fill with his own passion for reforming the morals of others. "You should feel," he told the Sixth, "like officers in the army or navy," by which he did not mean that they should develop a taste for drink and women, but that they should impose a severe and continuous discipline on the younger boys.

This they did, and with such vigour that at one time the public interest was aroused, but Dr. Arnold refused to be drawn into a debate on humanitarianism. "I do not choose," he said, "to discuss the thickness of praepostor's sticks or the greater or less blackness of a boy's bruises, for the amusement of all the readers of the newspapers."

His sermons in the school chapel concerned themselves exclusively with moral improvement. He could not even dismiss the boys to their holidays without wondering, with regard to the great mass of them, balanced as they were between good and evil, "what may be the effect produced upon them by the approaching vacation." The boys, or at least the praepostors, listened to these addresses, Dean Stanley tells us, "with their eyes fixed upon him, and their attention strained to the utmost to catch every word that he uttered."

V. RUGBY'S SONS

"RUGBY'S sons take to Oxford a different character than those of other institutions, more thoughtful, conscious of duty, and obligation."

That was the view of Arnold's work at Rugby, as seen by an admirer. Those who did not admire Dr. Arnold expressed the same view, in another form. In his essay on Matthew Arnold, Swinburne calls Matthew "David, the son of Goliath" and confesses himself unable to understand "how such a graft could ever have been set by the head-gardener of the main hotbed of Philistine saplings now flourishing in England."

Swinburne would naturally be out of sympathy with Dr. Arnold, but his view coincides with that of Charles Henry Pearson, a Fellow of Oriel and later Education Minister in Victoria, who had been at Rugby under Arnold. "The doctor," Pearson writes in his "Memoirs," "has been extravagantly overpraised. He cannot be credited with abolishing exclusively classical studies, and introducing History, French, and German; he did not originate the teaching of foreign languages and he had them badly taught."

Arnold, Pearson continues, had "a dangerous propensity to impel his pupils into Holy Orders. . . . I I cannot doubt that Clough, almost the ablest of

Arnold's pupils, though he escaped ordination, owed much of his morbid scrupulosity to the Rugby influence. . . . Arnold's pupils lived in a state of priggishness. They were taught to be always feeling their moral muscles, always careful about their schoolfellows' morality, and always mindful of the high mission which they took with them into the world as Rugby boys.

"Rugby was known at Oxford as 'the disagreeable school.'"

A few quotations from a school magazine. "The Rugby Miscellany," produced at Rugby shortly after Dr. Arnold's death, and written by the boys themselves, will illustrate what Rugby was like after Arnold had worked his will upon it, and may also explain why Oxford did not feel at ease with Rugbaeans.

1. From an article entiled "Eton, Winchester, and Rugby." "The Etonian . . . has a decided *manner*, and this manner, generally speaking, corresponds to that prevalent among the higher circles. In Society, this gives him an advantage over the Rugbaean, who has generally no manner: but even in this last fact there is a significance; where there is no manner, the ground is open for the formation of the best manner, and we think in a very few instances a manner has been developed in Rugbaeans of a higher order than that of the Etonian."

2. From an Editorial.

"We love but little to see boys assuming a gravity beyond the measure of their years, for we are persuaded that while for the most part they gain nothing in strength either of thought or expression, they lose by affectation much of that freshness which ought to be peculiarly their own. And yet there is a seriousness, which even in boys is not affected; such seriousness, we mean, as is called forth in us by a steady retrospect of the past. . . .

A year and a half between the age of seventeen and twenty-one is no common period. It is then most probably that must come that sifting of our early ideas and feelings which they must undergo, if our opinions are ever to be aught than the maxims of a debasing bigotry, or our faith higher than the grovelling unchangeableness of instinct."

3. From another Editorial.

"There are sundry facetiæ as old as the days of Hierocles to the effect, that all who wish to swim, must first take the inaugural plunge."

4. From a poem, entitled "Your Schoolboy Friendships, what are they?"

This quotation is not quite in key with the rest; but it would be a pity to omit it.

> "To know there is one faithful breast
>   Though all beside forsake us,
> Where we our weary heads may rest
>   And sleep till pleasure wake us:
> One breast that answers to our own
>   As brother's should to brother's;
> Such knowledge ne'er can be o'erthrown
>   By all the scoffs of others. . . .

"When to dull eyes we weakest seem,
  We feel most truly human,
Living in love's ecstatic dream,
  More dear than love of woman."

THE school whose destinies Arnold really hankered to direct was Christendom. His ambition was to Christianize politics, to make the Church that is, "not a subordinate but a sovereign society." With this end in view, he designed a work on "Christian politics," "to embrace an historical sketch of the pretended conversion of the kingdom of the world to the kingdom of Christ in the fourth and fifth centuries, which I look upon as one of the greatest tours d'adresse that Satan ever played, except his invention of popery. I mean that by inducing kings and nations to conform nominally to Christianity, and then to get into their hands the direction of Christian society, he has in a great measure succeeded in keeping out the peculiar principles of that society from any extended sphere of operation, and insuring the ascendancy of his own. One real conversion there seems to have been, that of the Anglo-Saxons; but that he soon succeeded in corrupting."

Satan's tours d'adresse having placed insuperable barriers between himself and the headmastership of Christendom, Dr. Arnold read the future with profound misgiving. "My sense of the evils of the times, and to what prospects I am bringing up my children is overwhelmingly bitter," he writes.

The disordered state of the world seemed to him to

forebode the end of an era in the history of mankind. "The termination of the Jewish αἰών in the first century, and of the Roman αἰών in the fifth and sixth, were each marked by the same concurrence of calamities, wars, tumults, pestilences, earthquakes, etc., all marking the time of God's peculiar season of visitations."

Various schemes for staving off God's threatened visitation occurred to him from time to time. He approved of the French Revolution, because it had abolished feudalism, and given France "small sub-divided properties, and general intelligence and an absence of aristocratical manners and distinction," but he did not desire a similar revolution in England, not caring to risk losing "my seven children and a good house (to put it on no other ground)."

He felt, however, that something ought to be done. "The old state of things is gone past recall, and all the efforts of all the Tories cannot save it, but they may by their folly, as they did in France, get us a wild democracy, or a military despotism in the room of it, instead of letting it change quietly into what is merely a new modification of the old state. . . . I want to get up a real Poor Man's Magazine, which should not bolster up abuses and veil iniquities, nor prose to the poor as to children."

This, and other similar projects, were never realized. Rugby, till his early death at forty-seven, continued to be the sole channel of his reforming energy; hence the puzzled look, which Lytton Strachey speaks of, discernible in his blunt honest face. When Stanley left

Rugby for Oxford, and wrote to Dr. Arnold to say how much he loved the place, the doctor replied that he, too, loved the place, adding "My love for any place, or person, or institution, is exactly the measure of my desire to reform them." He was interested, that is, neither in men nor in institutions for their own sakes, but only as material to be reshaped according to his private ideas of what was required.

MATT was born at Laleham on December 24th, 1822, I have tried hard to visualize Matt as infant and child, but without success. His contribution to "the rare, the unbroken, the almost awful happiness" of Dr. Arnold's domestic life evades me.

It is not only that external facts are wanting. There is no internal evidence from his poetry that he felt his early years with the intensity of most imaginative writers. In 1852 he wrote to his mother from Derby: "I looked affectionately in the bright morning towards Fledborough (Matt's grandfather was vicar of Fledborough); my recollections of it are the only approach I have to a memory of a golden age."

Had he been oftener at Fledborough in his early years, and so less continually involved in the awful felicity of his father's home life, he would have understood many things to which he remained insensible throughout his life. Above all, he would have understood Wordsworth's "Ode," his criticism of which might have been, and in a sense actually was, written by his father.

"Even the 'intimations' of the famous 'Ode,'" he writes, ". . . the idea of the high instincts and affections coming out in childhood, testifying of a divine home recently left, and fading away as one's life proceeds—this idea, of undeniable beauty as a play of fancy, has itself not the character of poetic truth of the best kind; it has no real solidity. . . . In many people, perhaps the majority of educated persons, the love of nature is nearly imperceptible at ten years old, but strong and operative at thirty."

Clearly, at Laleham, no quarter was given to

> "Those obstinate questionings
> Of sense and outward things,
> Fallings from us, vanishings;
> Blank misgivings of a Creature
> Moving about in worlds not realized,
> High instincts before which our mortal nature,
> Did tremble like a guilty thing surprised."

In a letter to his mother, written in his late twenties, he describes the country round Laleham. The description is matter-of-fact though quite charming, and with no hint in it of the emotion stirred in him by the distant sight of Fledborough. "Yesterday I was at Chertsey, the poetic town of our childhood, as opposed to the practical, historical Staines: it is *across* the river, reached by no bridges and roads, but by the primitive ferry; the meadow-path, the Abbey river with its wooden bridge and the narrow lane by the old wall; and, itself the stillest of country towns backed by St. Ann's, leads nowhere but to the heaths and pines of Surrey."

IT was towards the close of 1819 that Dr. Arnold wrote to one of his friends—"Don Juan has been with me for some weeks."

I imagine that the baleful visitor muttered some incantation or other as he left the doctor's house. I seem to hear him urging the Goddess Lubricity to weave her spells round the doctor's first man child. At any rate, in the little that is directly recorded about Matt in his boyhood and youth there is certainly a hint of something in his nature not in keeping with the traditions of Laleham and Rugby. When he came back to Rugby for the holidays from his private school he paraded "an astonishingly copious repertory of schoolboy slang before his brothers and sisters." At Winchester, at the end of his first year, he was "adjudged to have obtained the palm of rhetoric over the whole school by his declamation of the last speech of Marino Faliero in Byron's drama." Then there was another incident during his short stay at Winchester, the interpretation of which, however, is doubtful. At breakfast one day he remarked to his housemaster that he found his school work very easy to dispose of. After breakfast his affronted schoolfellows led him out to "cloister-peelings," a punishment in which the victim was pelted in the presence of the whole school with "pontos," round missiles made of the crumb of new bread. It is difficult to decide how far, in this incident, he figures as his father's son and how far as a Byronic hero in embryo; perhaps, one might say, as a not quite happy blend of the two.

After one year at Winchester, he was removed in 1847 to Rugby, where, as the son of the headmaster, he would be immune from the Rugbaean equivalent of "cloister-peelings." In 1840 he was awarded an open scholarship at Balliol, going into residence in the following year.

Before leaving Rugby, he won the prize poem. The subject was Alaric at Rome, and we are shown Alaric musing on the Capitoline Hill, in a mood of subdued Byronic melancholy.

> "Perchance his wandering heart was far away,
> Lost in dim memories of his early home."

There is a hint, too, rather surprising in a man of Alaric's stamp, of that elevated self-dissatisfaction to which, when listening to Dr. Arnold's sermons, his favourite praepostors often yielded themselves:

> "Energies wasted, unimprovèd hours,
> The saddening vision of departed days."

I WILL conclude this necessarily meagre sketch of Matt's early years with a quotation from a letter he wrote to his wife, shortly after their marriage. A man's letters to his wife should not, as a rule, be used in evidence against him. They are apt to express a less abounding sense of the joy of life than the writers actually feels. But the flatness of the following passage faithfully reproduces a corresponding flatness in Matt's childhood and boyhood:

"It would be such a pleasure to go over with you the places I knew from the time I was eight till I was twenty. Then all the people who remember me and my family would be *so* pleased to see you. You would like to see where I used to play with my brothers and sisters, and walk with the governess, and bathe, and learn dancing and many other things."

This, and the two quotations previously given, contain practically all that Matt has to say in his letters about the first nineteen years of his life. During his most impressionable years he was almost continuously under his father's eye to the immense impoverishment of his experience, and therefore of his poetic resources. He never touched either extreme of life, neither in his childhood seeing the earth apparelled in celestial light, nor in his school or later years coming into contact with the brutal side of human nature. Hence the unsatisfactory and often irritating effect both of his work and of his personality on those whose experience of life had been less comfortable than his. There is a letter from Froude to Clough, written in 1849, which illustrates this. Froude, as a schoolboy at Westminster, had been starved, repeatedly thrashed, made drunk on brandy, wakened at night by the burning ends of cigars, had his clothes and books stolen, and been beaten by his father for pawning them.

"I admire Matt to a very great extent," he writes to Clough, "only I don't see what business he has to parade his calmness, and lecture us on resignation, when he has never known what a storm is, and doesn't know what to resign himself to. I think he only knows the shady side of nature out of books."

Except between Rugby and his marriage, Matt never absorbed life with any freedom. What is of value in his poetry is derived almost exclusively from his contact with life during this period; and even so this contact was regrettably restricted by the dead hand of his father, to whose maiming effect on himself and on so many others he never ceased to pay grateful tribute.

"He carried so many others with him in his hand," Matt wrote to his mother, when he was thirty-three, "and saved them, if they would let him, along with himself"; and in "Rugby Chapel" he figures his father as a shepherd and himself, Clough, Stanley, and the rest as sheep; which indeed they were.

"But thou wouldst not *alone*
Be saved, my father! *alone*
Conquer and come to thy goal,
Leaving the rest in the wild.
We were weary, and we
Fearful, and we in our march
Fain to drop down and to die.
Still thou turned'st, and still
Gavest the weary thy hand.
. . . . To us thou wast still
Cheerful and helpful and firm!
Therefore to thee it was given
Many to save with thyself;
And at the end of thy day,
O faithful shepherd! to come,
Bringing thy sheep in thy hand."

X. OXFORD: GEORGE SAND

ARNOLD went up to Oxford in 1841. The chief authority, outside his own poetry, for Matt's springtime of life and joy is Mrs. Humphry Ward.

Mrs. Humphry Ward published a volume of reminiscences after the war, under the title of "A Writer's Recollections." She was able, as the niece of Matthew Arnold, and the daughter of Thomas, who was perhaps Matt's favourite brother, to supply a good deal of information about Matt and the Arnolds generally.

In 1857, after his election to the Professorship of Poetry at Oxford, Matt wrote to his brother Tom, Mrs. Ward's father, "You alone of my brothers are associated with that life at Oxford, the *freest* and most delightful part, perhaps, of my life, when with you and Clough and Walrond I shook off the bonds and formalities of the place, and enjoyed the spring of life and that unforgotten Oxfordshire and Berkshire country."

Matt and Tom and Clough, Mrs. Ward tells us, together discovered George Sand, Emerson, Carlyle and Wilhelm Meister, and were endlessly excited by them, and especially by George Sand. After Dr. Arnold, and that is perhaps the most favourable thing to be said of his methods, almost anything must have seemed like debauchery. Even at the close of his life, Matt still thrilled to his first memories of George Sand. "Days of 'Valentine,' days of 'Lèlia,'" he exclaims in a late essay on George Sand, "days never to return! They are gone, we shall read the books no more, and yet how ineffaceable is their impression! How the sentences from George Sand's works of that period still linger in our memory and haunt the ear with their cadences! Grandiose and moving, they come, those cadences, like the sighing of the wind through the forest, like the breaking of the waves on the seashore;" and he goes on to quote a long passage from "Lèlia," ending, "For ten thousand years, as the sole answer to my cries, as the sole comfort in my agony, I hear astir, over this earth accurst, the despairing sob of impotent agony. For ten thousand years I have cried in infinite space: *Truth! Truth!* For ten thousand years infinite space keeps answering me: *Desire! Desire!*"

How did George Sand's liberal views of love strike Matt and Tom and Arthur Clough and Walrond? In that unforgotten Oxfordshire and Berkshire country, the bonds and formalities of the place shaken off, and Rugby some counties away, did Matt, coughing a little tentatively, find a certain purifying unction in George Sand's treatment of adultery?

"You recall the passage, Arthur? It is when Jacques' wife, Fernande, has left him for Octave. She cries, don't you recollect? 'Oh, my dear Octave, we will never pass the night together without first kneeling down and praying for Jacques.'"

"Unsound," Tom mutters, from Clough's other side.

"Yes, I suppose so. Unsound!" and Matthew sighs.

I place Clough between the Arnold brothers because he would wish to talk, and, in a less degree, listen to Matt, while having Tom, whom he preferred, by his side. Walrond is lost to me, a vague figure at one or other end of the quartette, whom Carlyle, were he writing this book, would wonder at for a moment, that such an intrinsically dim personage should still walk the earth in these latter days, even though in so phantom-wise and all ways attenuated a shape. At whom, gesticulating inaudibilities, one glance shall suffice.

More than a single glance, however, may be spared to Tom Arnold and to Clough. Tom seems to have had no Byronic taint in his nature, and to have reacted less immediately against Rugby than Matt. While at Oxford he remained a liberal, and, like his father, was repelled by Newman and the Tractarian Movement. From Oxford he went to New Zealand and the change of scene unsettled him. He begat Mrs. Humphry Ward and he reacted against Dr. Arnold's politics and religion. He was "struck" one Sunday, Mrs. Ward tells us, "by the authoritative tone of the First Epistle of Peter. What justified such a tone?" Then he came across a life of Saint Brigit of Sweden, and sent to England for The Tracts for the Times. These did his business for him, and when he returned to England, he placed himself in Newman's hands. "How strange it seems," Newman wrote to him. "What a world this is! I knew your father a little, and I really think I never had any unkind feeling towards him."

~ THYRSIS ~
(Arthur Hugh Clough)
"But Thyrsis of his own will went away"

That Clough preferred Tom to Matt seems to be shown in his correspondence, which contains many letters to Tom, and also to J. N. Simpkinson and the Reverend J. P. Gell, names of fading significance for the present generation, but none to Matt; though this in itself is not conclusive evidence as Matt may not have kept Clough's letters. When Clough died, Matt wrote of him to his mother as "one of the few persons who ever made a deep impression upon me," but I can find no evidence that friendship with Clough, or anyone else, counted for much with Arnold. As far as Clough is concerned, Froude, in the letter I have quoted, would hardly have expressed himself as he did, had Matt and Clough been very close friends. Even in "Thyrsis," the monody Arnold wrote to commemorate Clough's death, what depth of feeling it contains springs from Arnold's own melancholy, not from regret for Clough. Compare, for example, these two stanzas, in the first of which he recalls the expeditions they took together, and in the second expresses his own disillusionment with life and growing desire for rest.

"Where is the girl, who by the boatman's door,
Above the locks, above the boating throng,
Unmoor'd our skiff when through the Wytham flats,
Red loosestrife and blond meadowsweet among
And darting swallows and light water-gnats,
We track'd the shy Thames shore?
Where are the mowers, who, as the tiny swell
Of our boat passing heaved the river-grass,
Stood with suspended scythe to see us pass?
They all are gone, and thou art gone as well!"

and:

> "And long the way appears, that seem'd so short
> To the less practised eye of sanguine youth;
> And high the mountain tops in cloudy air,
> The mountain-tops where is the throne of truth.
> Tops in life's morning-sun so bright and bare!
>   Unbreachable the fort
> Of the long-batter'd world uplifts its wall;
> And strange and vain the earthly turmoil grows,
> And near and real the charm of thy repose,
> And night as welcome as a friend would fall."

Apart from two lyrics, "Say not the struggle naught availeth," and "As ships becalmed," Clough wrote nothing that has survived till to-day. It is difficult to see why Arnold should have been deeply impressed by him, unless because he intermittently shared Clough's vague hope that everything would turn out all right in the long run.

"We," Clough writes,

> "Must still believe, for still we hope
> That in a world of larger scope,
> What here is faithfully begun,
> Will be completed, not undone."

Clough had naturally some sense of humour, but the shape in which it issues, after his mangling at the hands of Dr. Arnold, is rather unnerving.

"Good heavens!" he writes to a friend who had criticized his "Amours de Voyage." "Don't be afraid. You are a very gentle beast, and of a good conscience, and roar me like any sucking-dove. You're a funny creature, my dear old fellow; if one don't sing you a ballant, or read you a philosophical sermonette, if one don't talk about the gowans or truth, you're not pleased."

G EORGE SAND and Goethe and the other secu-
lar writers, who in his undergraduate period
inflamed Matt's imagination with visions of worldly
happiness and triumphs and tragedy, never altogether
overlaid the impression of Dr. Arnold's training, which,
though the form it took would have been incomprehen-
sible to Dr. Arnold, survived in Matt's strong attraction
towards Newman. In Newman, Matt, frightened by the
onset of life, found the spiritual help he needed. As
late as 1872, he wrote to Newman to tell him that
Goethe, Wordsworth and Sainte-Beuve, Newman had
been one of the four from whom he was conscious of
having learnt "habits, methods, ruling ideas," and in
his lecture on Emerson, delivered towards the close
of his life, he returns to his undergraduate memory
of Newman in a passage as deeply felt as the one I
have quoted above about George Sand.

"Forty years ago he was in the very prime of life;
he was preaching in St. Mary's pulpit every Sunday;
he seemed about to transform and renew what was for
us the most national and natural institution in the
world, the Church of England. Who could resist the
charm of that spiritual apparition, gliding in the dim
afternoon light through the aisles of St. Mary's, rising
into the pulpit, and then, in the most entrancing of

voices, breaking the silence with words and thoughts which were a religious music—subtle, sweet, mournful? I seem to hear him still, saying: 'After the fever of life, after wearinesses and sicknesses, fighting and despondings, languor and fretfulness, struggling and succeeding; after all the changes and chances of this troubled, unhealthy state—at length comes death, at length the white throne of God, at length the beatific vision.' "

Arnold was never tempted to follow Newman to Rome; nor either in youth or age was he attracted by the imitation Catholicism of one section of the Anglican Church, as is shown by his reference in "Westminster Abbey" to

> "Folly revived, re-furbished sophistries,
> And pullulating rites externe and vain."

It seems to me that Newman's chief attraction for Arnold, at any rate in his youth, was his combination of purity and aloofness from life with poetic feeling. Whether Newman's poetry unsupported by his character would have charmed Arnold, a careful study of the passage quoted above, with its vague and hackneyed phrases, makes doubtful.

XII. "EFFUSIVE OXONOLATRY"

IN 1873 John Campbell Shairp published a poem called "Balliol Scholars, 1840–1843," in which he described Arnold as follows:

> "The one, wide-welcomed for a father's fame,
> Entered with free bold step that seemed to claim
> Fame for itself, nor on another lean.
>
> So full of power, yet blithe and debonair,
> Rallying his friends with pleasant banter gay,
> Or half-a-dream chaunting with jaunty air
> Great words of Goethe, catch of Béranger."

A friend, writing in the *Times* after Arnold's death, gives a similar picture of Matt as an undergraduate— "His perfect self-possession, the sallies of his ready wit, the humorous turn that he could give to any subject that he handled, his gaiety, exuberance, versatility, audacity and unfailing command of words made him one of the most popular and successful undergraduates Oxford has ever known."

Neither of these portraits smacks too poignantly of reality, but they suggest the Byronic element which blossomed out, within the limits of a decent exuberance, as soon as Matt had escaped from Rugby.

They explain, too, in their picture of Matt for once comparatively unrestrained, his "effusive Oxonolatry," as Swinburne called it. Men of genius, as a rule, have had little respect or affection for their universities; in support of which the following names occur to me: Dryden, Swift, Gibbon, Goethe, Heine, Wordsworth, Shelley, Tennyson, Swinburne, Landor and Burton. Matt, even, had one lucid moment, in a letter to his wife, written in 1854. "I am much struck with the apathy and poorness of the people here (Oxford), as they now strike me, and their petty, pottering habits, compared with the students of Paris, or Germany, or even London." But he had not been long married when he wrote this, and still had fresh in his mind, as a standard of life by which to judge existence at Oxford, the epoch between Oxford and his marriage. As the years passed, and life became increasingly dreary, Oxford resumed the fascination which had dazzled him when he came to it from Rugby; moving him, in the famous passage from the preface to the "Essays in Criticism," to an abandonment as rapturous as Titania's embracing Bottom.

"Adorable dreamer, whose heart has been so romantic! who hast given thyself so prodigally, given thyself to sides to heroes not mine, only never to the Philistines! home of lost causes, and forsaken beliefs, and unpopular names, and impossible loyalties! What example could ever so inspire us to keep down the Philistine in ourselves. . . ."

Anyone unacquainted with the history of Oxford would hardly guess, after this eloquence, that apart from backing the wrong horse in the struggle between

Charles I. and Parliament, and as a result suffering a
certain amount of inconvenience; to which inconsiderable crucifixion one may add some bickering, the details
of which have become vague to me, between Magdalen
College and James II., Oxford, less from vigilance than
from drowsiness, has kept itself throughout the centuries comfortably disentangled from the social and
political disturbances of the age.

Someone unacquainted with the facts would rather
suppose, after reading Arnold's apostrophe, that under
Elizabeth droves of Catholic dons were herded to
drown in the Cher, that under Cromwell college after
college was stormed and the learned garrisons put to the
sword, that under the Georges a *battue* of Jacobite dons
formed the weekly diversion of mercenaries imported
from Hesse and Hanover, and that in the Hungry
'Forties a handful of devoted professors perished to
the last man defending the priceless manuscripts of the
Bodleian against the uncivilized frenzy of a maddened
proletariat.

In "Culture and Anarchy," which appeared two or
three years after "Essays in Criticism," Arnold, who
must in the interval have wondered from time to time
what exactly this apostrophe of his meant, tried to make
it convincing to himself and to others by restating it in
a more subdued key.

"We in Oxford, brought up amidst the beauty and
sweetness of that beautiful place, have not failed to
seize one truth—the truth that beauty and sweetness are
essential characters of a complete human perfection.

When I insist on this, I am all in the faith and tradition of Oxford. I say boldly that this our sentiment for beauty and sweetness, our sentiment against hideousness and rawness, has been at the bottom of our attachment to so many beaten causes, of our opposition to so many triumphant movements. . . . We have not won our political battles, we have not carried our main points, we have not stopped our adversaries' advance, we have not marched victoriously with the modern world; but we have told silently upon the mind of the country, we have prepared currents of feeling which sap our adversaries' position when it seems gained, we have kept up our communications with the future."

In this apologia even the admissions of failure are too flattering. The political battles lost by Oxford, the main points she has failed to carry, the adversaries whose advance she has been unable to check, are all phantasms of Matt's thwarted Cæsarism. Neither Oxford nor Matt was cast for a part of any importance in the affairs of the world. Oxford, comfortably off, with its term times sufficiently occupied to make its vacations a pleasant change, has always realized this truth. Matt, unfortunately for the work he was competent to do, did not realize it.

In support of his claim that Oxford, while failing in everything it undertook, had at any rate "told silently upon the mind of the country" Matt asks us to "look at the course of the great movement which shook Oxford to its centre thirty years ago! It was directed, as anyone who reads Dr. Newman's 'Apology' may see,

against what in one word may be called 'Liberalism.'
Liberalism prevailed; it was the appointed force to
do the work of the hour; it was necessary, it was inevitable that it should prevail. . . . But what was it,
this Liberalism, as Dr. Newman saw it, and as it really
broke the Oxford movement? It was the great middle-
class Liberalism which had for the cardinal points of its
belief the Reform Bill of 1832 and local self-govern-
ment in politics; in the social sphere, free trade, unrestricted competition, and the making of large industrial fortunes; in the religious sphere the Dissidence of
Dissent and the Protestantism of the Protestant religion. . . .

"Where is this great force of Philistinism now? It is
thrust into the second rank, it has become a power of
yesterday, it has lost the future."

And this is due to Newman? Well, not exactly, but:

"Who will estimate how much the currents of feeling
created by Dr. Newman's movements, the keen desire
for beauty and sweetness which it nourished, the deep
aversion which it manifested to the hardness and vulgarity of middle-class liberalism, the strong light it
turned on the hideous and grotesque illusions of middle-class Protestantism—who will estimate how much
all these contributed to swell the tide of secret dissatisfaction which has mined the ground under the self-
confident liberalism of the last thirty years?"

Arnold would have done better to leave his original
apostrophe to Oxford un-annotated.

Since Arnold wrote "Culture and Anarchy," there

have been two other Oxford movements, Canon Barnett's Toynbee Hall, with its Christian Socialism as a bun to the proletarian bear, and Oscar Wilde's Aesthetic Movement, whose frontal attack on British Philistinism was itself surprised in its undefended rear by the alert officers of the law. But even when we add the names of Canon Barnett and Oscar Wilde to Newman's, it is hard to feel impressed by Oxford's contribution to the social, moral and intellectual development of the modern world.

XIII. THE UNKNOWN YEARS

I AM deeply aware that so far neither Matt nor I have found each other congenial companions. But I believe our relations are about to improve, if only for a time. I have been unable to sympathize with him in his attitude to Dr. Arnold and to Rugby, to Dr. Newman and to Oxford. Yet Matt, after all, was a poet, and now as I approach his brief poetic period, and the experiences out of which it flowered, I believe we shall find each other more sympathetic. My investigations into his personal history will jar on him at times, but he will recognize that a George Russell inevitably begets his contrary, and in his astonishment that I should have been begotten by George Russell, he will forget his own injuries.

In his finals Matt obtained only a second class, instead of the first which is, very rightly, expected of scholars. Matt had, however, distinguished himself enough already by winning the Hertford, and the Newdigate, the latter for a poem on Cromwell. In this poem Cromwell, about to embark for America, is rapt in a trance in which he sees, among other things and persons, Charles I., whom a doubtful legend reports to have once played with Cromwell when they were both children.

"He, too, was there—it was the princely boy,
The child-companion of his childish joy!"

In spite of this, and in spite of his failure to get a
first, Matt was elected a Fellow of Oriel in 1845.

During the next two years, except for a short period,
of which there is no record, as a master at Rugby, Matt
seems to have been more his own master than at any
other period of his life. How did he occupy himself?

The author of the biographical article in the *Times*,
from which I have already quoted, narrates that during
the early part of 1846 Clough used every Sunday to
entertain at breakfast a small party of friends, consist-
ing of Matthew, his brother of University, and Theo-
dor Walrond; and that practically exhausts what this
fastidious artist in biography has to tell us about these
two years.

George Russell, naturally, publishes no letters of
Matt's during this period, and Mrs. Humphry Ward
gives us no definite information, though I shall presently quote from her some interesting references to
Matt made round about this time by members of his
family and others.

Fortunately, in one of his late essays, "The French
Play in London," Matt lets fall a sentence which
lightens some of the obscurity of this period. He tells
us that in his youth he followed the great actress Rachel
from England to Paris, and never missed one night
for a whole season at the theatre where Rachel was
playing.

The fact that Matt spent a whole season in Paris

in a state of excitement over an actress would be taken by many as conclusive evidence that he had entirely jettisoned the philosophy of conduct learnt at or across his father's knee. It seems to me, however, more probable that Matt, at any rate while in Paris, found in Rachel's acting a sufficient assuagement of the worldly, theatrical and Byronic element in his nature. I picture him, each night, after the theatre, walking home down the Bois de Boulogne with an air of courtly abstraction very baffling to the girls on patrol duty there, who would see in him not a sheep reposing in the ghostly hand of Dr. Arnold, but an elegant young dandy with carefully trimmed side-whiskers.

Another view of Matt at this period, much fuller, though no more significant, is given us in Matt's essay on George Sand, from which I have already quoted.

George Sand, after an exhaustive experience of love in the usual sense of that word, became a prophetess of love in the diluted form of a concern for the general welfare of humanity. It is on this aspect of her that Matt dwells longest in his essay, written when he was fifty-five. She is to be valued chiefly, he thinks, for her "aspiration towards a purged and renewed human society."

But life, even to Matt, seemed at one time a woman to be loved, not a broken-down machine to be tinkered with; and it is because George Sand was associated with this time of expectation that he writes of her with such emotion.

~ GEORGE SAND ~

He struck a chill to her Heart

"It seems to me but the other day," he begins his essay, "that I saw her, yet it was in the August of 1846, more than thirty years ago. I saw her in her own Berry, at Nohant, where her childhood and youth were passed, where she returned to live after she became famous, where she died and has now her grave. There must be many who, after reading her books, have felt the same desire which in those days of my youth, in 1846, took me to Nohant—the desire to see the country and the places of which the books that so charmed us were full."

The way he returns to and lingers on the year 1846 is worth noting. "Those old provinces, the centre of France," he continues, "primitive and slumbering; Berry, La Marche, Bourbonnais; those sites and streams in them, of name once so indifferent to us, but to which George Sand gave such a music for our ear—La Châtre, Ste. Sévère, the Vallée Noire, the Indre, the Creuse: how many a reader of George Sand must have desired, as I did, after frequenting them so much in thought, fairly to set eyes upon them!"

He then recounts, with the minute detail of a man remembering a period of great happiness, his journey by rail, diligence and foot to the country of Jeanne," one of George Sand's novels.

"That day and the next I wandered through a silent country of healthy and ferny *landes,* a region of granite boulders, holly and broom, of copse, wood and great chestnut trees; a region of broad light, and fresh breezes, and wide horizons. I visited the Pierres Jaun-âtres. I stood at sunset on the platform of Toulx St. Croix, by the scrawled and almost effaced stone lions—a relic, it is said, of the English rule—and gazed on the blue mountains of Auvergne filling the distance, and, southeastward of them, in a still further and fainter distance, on what seemed to be the mountains of Le Puy in the high valley of the Loire."

From Broussat he wrote to George Sand "a letter conveying to her, in bad French, the homage of a youthful and enthusiastic foreigner." George Sand replied with an invitation to Nohant.

"The midday breakfast at Nohant was not yet over when I reached the house, and I found a large party assembled. I entered with some trepidation, as well I might, considering how I had got there; but the simplicity of Madame Sand's manner put me at ease in a moment. She named some of those present; amongst them were her son and daughter, the Maurice and Solange so familiar to us from her books, and Chopin with his wonderful eyes. . . . Madame Sand made me sit by her. She conversed of the country through which I had been wandering, of the Berry peasants and their mode of life, of Switzerland, whither I was going; she touched politely, by a few questions and remarks, upon England and things and persons English—upon Oxford and Cambridge, Byron, Bulwer. . . .

"After breakfast she led the way into the garden, asked me a few kind questions about myself and my plans, gathered a flower or two and gave them to me, shook hands heartily at the gate, and·I saw her no more."

George Sand's impression of Matt has been recorded. He made on her, she said, "*l'effet d'un Milton jeune et voyageant.*" Had he made on her the effect of a Byron or a Bulwer, the mighty woman who had ravished so many weeping men of genius would have added Matt to the list of her victims, to the enrichment by ecstasy and remorse, rage and despair, of all his future work. I hear a strangled cry breaking the midnight calm of Nohant—"Father, where are you?"—but the shade of Dr. Arnold would have been powerless against the substance of George Sand.

These, however, are idle dreams. This purging and renewing experience was denied to Matt, and we must make the best of him as he is without wasting regrets on what he might have become.

Besides, it is probably true that everyone gets the experience he is qualified for. To Matt, tremulous and poignant longings in "a region of broad light, and fresh breezes, and wide horizons": to Alfred de Musset, etc., etc., the embraces of George Sand.

I have quoted at length from this essay on George Sand, as a man about to pick his way across a dangerous bog lingers on the last patch of firm land with a brooding appreciation of its solidity. George Russell himself, were he alive, could not deny that Matt in 1846 was in a romantic and over-excited frame of mind. So much is clearly established by his Parisian season at the shrine of Rachel and this pilgrimage to the country and the home of George Sand. But Russell and many others would decline, fretfully or firmly, according to their temperaments, to advance one foot into the region of inference that I propose now to traverse.

XIV. THE MAN AND THE WRITER

"WHY wish to know about the man? Haven't you
got his books? Aren't they all that matters?"
These are the questions that even nowadays, when the
Victorian tradition is supposed to be dead, are frequently
addressed to anyone who is curious about the personal
history of a writer. I have never seen them fully answered, and I think it would be as well to answer them
before I examine Matt's love story.

My first criticism of these questions is that they smack
of that Victorian preoccupation with art for art's sake
which enabled the readers of "David Copperfield" to
luxuriate in the domestic felicity of David and Agnes
and the three children of their ten years' marriage
without checking it by reference to the domestic infelic-
ity of Charles Dickens and Mrs. Charles Dickens and
the children, ten in number, of *their* ten years' marriage.

I choose this example because it was possible for
Dickens' readers, even during his lifetime, to test, had
they so wished, the relation between his life and his
books. When Dickens and his wife separated, Dickens
issued an official bulletin in his paper *Household
Words,* assuring the public, in effect, that the situation
was well in hand, and that the campaign for the estab-

lishment of universal domestic felicity would continue, as heretofore, under Dickens' personal direction. This bulletin was received with relief, and the public continued to read Dickens' books, after assuring themselves that it was only his writings with which they were concerned.

Naturally, it is impossible to assess the effect on the Victorians of their refusal to examine the relation between Dickens the man and Dickens the writer, but, as I have come across two examples of it myself, I assume there must be thousands of other equally interesting examples.

A friend of mine, V. C., having passed from Eton to Clifton, and having returned from Clifton to the home which he originally left to go to Eton, his father, a student of Dickens, recalled that at the close of "David Copperfield" all the characters who had failed to establish themselves in the Victorian social fabric left for Australia, where they at once found well-paid jobs or were married off to prosperous backwoodsmen, according to the nature of their requirements. V. C. was accordingly shipped to Australia, whence he returned within the year, having suffered considerable discomfort both on the outward and the homeward voyage. He was then sent to Texas, with instructions to be a cowboy. It may have occurred to V. C.'s father that cowboys frequently shot each other. It certainly occurred to V. C. I asked him if there was much shooting in the saloons. He replied that revolvers were used in some saloons, and not in others, and, in answer to a second question, he said he frequented those saloons only where revolvers were not used; adding that, when the usage of any particular saloon in the matter of revolvers was uncertain, he stayed away. On the whole, he had not cared for the life much, though he had liked the cowboys, friendly and simple men, and had found a certain interest each morning in counting the eggs laid during the previous night by the hens.

From Texas he returned to England, where he settled down on an allowance from his father.

In this instance, owing to V.C.'s imperturbable realism, everything ended happily. In the other instance, an exact imitation of the match-making debauches of Dickens' elderly satyrs, Pickwick, the Cheeryble Brothers, etc., had its sequel for the youthful victims a year or two later in the divorce courts.

I infer from these two instances that it is important to know about the man behind his books. If the picture of life which a writer gives can be shown to be at variance with his own experience and conduct the reader will be on his guard, and will not, for example, disperse all over the earth a son whose natural bent lies in the direction of living at home on unearned increment. It may be said that a man should test the reality of a book, not by inquiry into the private life of the author but by his own sense of reality; and this would be an argument of a sort if a sense of reality were more common than it is. But not only is it uncommon; even where it exists it needs perpetual nourishment, and one of the best means of nourishing it is by studying the interrelation of a man and his writings. The recent attempts to reconstruct the personality of Shakespeare (according to the Victorians a devoted husband) are deepening our understanding of the plays, and this deepened understanding is in its turn increasing our knowledge of the man.

The view that the private life of a man, whose work, whether in literature or elsewhere, has interested the world, should be opened to the public, is not, as is imagined by the fretful person I have quoted at the beginning of this entry, a specimen of modern indecency. It was, still the Victorian era, the established view of civilized mankind, and answered to the instinctive feeling that a man's public work cannot be finally judged without reference to his character as shown in the ordinary relations of life.

If the Bible had been written in conformity with Victorian taste, the world would have known nothing of the circumstances that led up to the marriage of King David with the charming and popular widow of the late brevet colonel Uriah; and the denial of Christ by Peter would have been dismissed in an obscurely worded footnote as a piece of scandal undeserving detailed refutation.

I would conclude this entry with a few words of comfort to my fretful interlocutor. It was necessary to inform him that it was he, not I, who was in a morbid condition. Let me now explain to him the cause of his malady. Once he has grasped this, the malady itself should disappear.

Broadly speaking, there are two causes, and his condition may be due to one or to the other, or to an admixture of the two, since they are not always mutually exclusive.

The first cause is best expressed in Claudius' exclamation when he was informed that Hamlet had driven his sword through the curtain which concealed Polonius, and transfixed Polonius:

"It had been so with us had we been there."

My interlocutor, whom I shall call A., is not chiefly concerned about, say, Dickens. Were it established that Dickens was a cannibal at home and a white-slave trafficker in office hours, A. would express astonishment and concern, and might doubt if he could ever read Pickwick again with the old enjoyment; and that would be the extent of his suffering as far as Dickens was concerned. It is when he imagines himself in Dickens' place, exposed to the public view, that he is touched to the quick, either because his life contains an exciting scandal or two, or because it doesn't.

The second cause derives from the instinct of hero-worship, and is therefore much more excusable. A. finds life itself a tedious and petty business. The trivial imperfections of his own character disgust him, and he desires a vicarious satisfaction of his thwarted ideals in the contemplation of the unflawed and noble lives of great men. Therefore, he cannot bear to hear of any faults or weaknesses in them.

"Even if he was like that, isn't it a pity to be told about it? And, in any case, I for one refuse to believe that the man who wrote . . ."

It is a touching formula, but unsuitable for those who wish to strengthen their digestions.

XV. MARGUERITE

IN 1849 Arnold published his first volume of verse, "The Strayed Reveller and other Poems by A." In 1852, a year after his marriage, his second volume appeared, "Empedocles on Etna and other Poems by A."; and in the following year he brought out, under his own name, a new edition, in which "Empedocles" and a few small poems were omitted, but which contained some important additions, "Sohrab and Rustum," "The Scholar-Gypsy," "Requiescat" and "The Church of Brou."

These three volumes, the last of which appeared when he was just over thirty, contain nearly all his best work in poetry. Owing partly to his sincerity, and partly to his inability to see the world through anyone's eyes but his own, Arnold has revealed himself, allowing for the reticence imposed by his environment, very fully and explicitly in these three volumes, and especially in the poems inspired directly or indirectly by Marguerite.

The obscurity in which the piety of his family and friends has involved the period from 1845 to 1851 makes it impossible to fix the dates when most of the poems were composed. The second volume, which contains nearly all the poems written to Marguerite, appeared a year after his marriage, from which a George Russell might infer that these poems were pleasant exercises of fancy composed during Matt's honeymoon in the intervals between theological and political discussions with his bride. It is clear, however, from internal evidence that the bulk of these poems, at any rate, were written between 1846 and 1849, and were held over for publication until after his marriage. If he were engaged or hoping to be engaged to his future wife in 1849, Arnold would have felt the moment unpropitious for issuing a series of love poems to another woman.

I shall therefore take all the poems connected with his love for Marguerite together, before passing on to the poems deriving from other sources.

I am compelled to rely, in reconstructing Arnold's love story, entirely on the internal evidence of his poems, in spite of several attempts to find some external evidence to corroborate the internal. First of all, I secured, through a misapprehension on his part, an interview with a nephew of Arnold's. Our talk was friendly but impalpable, and we parted with a sense of estrangement owing to my asking him, at the close of our interview, not in malice but in sincere curiosity, whether he had ever met his uncle.

I then wrote to Mr. Aldous Huxley, and, at his suggestion, to Arnold's grandson, Mr. Arnold Whitridge, who confirmed Mr. Aldous Huxley's impression that all correspondence relating to these critical years had been destroyed at Fox How, Dr. Arnold's home in the Lake District, and the family headquarters.

Mr. Whitridge added that Dr. Arnold's correspondence had all been religiously preserved. I concluded, therefore, that the destruction of Matthew's correspondence was not an accidental by-product of a spring cleaning.

One might reasonably suspect a dire mystery behind all this concealment. Certainly with Burns or Heine or Verlaine, if their friends and family had elaborately fenced off four or five years in the life of any one of them from public observation, one would have to infer some extremely complicated form of iniquity. With Matt one need infer nothing more than that for a short time his visits to the Continent stirred misgivings at Fox How. He no doubt confided, or at any rate hinted at his love in letters to his favourite sister, Jane. His friends, too, Stanley, Clough and Walrond, must have known something, and shaken troubled heads.

It was probably in the August of 1846 that Matt first met Marguerite. The detail with which, thirty years later, he describes his journey through George Sand's country reflects a warmer glow than his meeting even with George Sand could have imparted to that country in retrospect. He tells us, too, in the account of his talk with George Sand, that he was on his way to Switzerland. "She conversed of the country through which I had been wandering, of the Berry peasants and their mode of life, of Switzerland, whither I was going."

It is easy to establish where he and Marguerite met. In "The Terrace at Berne," the concluding poem of the "Switzerland" series, written ten years after the others, he puts Thun as the scene of his love-affair beyond dispute.

> "Ten years!—and to my waking eye
> Once more the roofs of Berne appear;
> The rocky banks, the terrace high,
> The stream!—and do I linger here?
>
> "The clouds are on the Oberland,
> The Jungfrau snows look faint and far;
> But bright are those green fields at hand,
> And through those fields comes down the Aar.
>
> "And from the blue twin-lakes it comes,
> Flows by the town, the churchyard fair;
> And 'neath the garden-walk it hums,
> The house!—and is my Marguerite there?"

The "blue twin-lakes" are Brienz and Thun. The Aar passes through both these lakes, and Thun is the town through which it flows on issuing from the second lake. A pedant might urge that there is nothing in the verse I quote to prove that the Aar had not flowed through the town of Thun first before flowing through Matt's town, which would therefore be some miles down stream from the lake itself. This objection is disposed of in two lines from another poem:

> "Again I see my bliss at hand,
> The town, the lake, are here."

Across the lake, looking eastward from Thun, rise beyond lesser ranges of mountains the peaks of the

～ THE LAKE OF THUN ～
(From a Contemporary Engraving)
The scene of Matthew's Love Story

Berner Oberland, the Jungfrau, Mönch, Eiger, Shreck-horn, and Wetterhorn. Arnold is always precise in his descriptions, and the following lines, taken in conjunction with those already quoted, could hardly be twisted to refer to any place but Thun.

> "Ye storm-winds of Autumn!
> Who rush by, who shake
> The window, and ruffle
> The gleam-lighted lake;
> Who cross to the hill-side
> Thin-sprinkled with farms,
> Where the high woods strip sadly
> Their yellowing arms.
> Ye are bound for the mountains!
> Ah! with you let me go,
> Where your cold distant barrier,
> The vast range of snow,
> Through the loose clouds lifts dimly
> Its white peaks in air.
> How deep is their stillness!
> Ah, would I were there!"

Marguerite, though, as will appear, not the wife whom Fox How would have chosen for Matthew, was also not the kind of girl with whom a chance encounter entangles a youthful poet in his holidays. I have heard it suggested that she was a waitress, a singer at a café chantant, or a general aid at an inn. I am happy to be able to associate myself with the shade of George Russell in repelling these suggestions.

She was, I think, a governess or a companion in a family that was living in Thun; or she may have been a teacher of French, living in apartments. In any case, it is clear that she was not a person of independent means, and therefore not a gentlewoman in the strict Victorian sense.

This inference is strengthened by Arnold's statement that she was French. Thun is in German Switzerland, and a French girl would hardly be living there for a long period except to impart her language. That she was what is technically known as a lady companion, and lived on terms of social equality with her employer, seems to be implied in the term "A Dream," which I think disposes of the possibility that she was living on her own.

> "Was it a dream? We sail'd, I thought we sail'd,
> Martin and I, down a green Alpine stream,
> Border'd each bank with pines . . .
> Swiss chalets glitter'd on the dewy slopes . . .
> We shot beneath the cottage with the stream,
> On the brown, rude-carved balcony, two forms
> Came forth—Olivia's, Marguerite! and thine.
> Clad were they both in white, flowers in their breast;
> Straw hats bedecked their heads, with ribbons blue,
> Which danc'd, and on their shoulders, fluttering, play'd.
> They saw us, they conferr'd; their bosoms heaved,
> And more than mortal impulse filled their eyes."

It is unnecessary to speculate who Martin was. He may have been Wyndham Slade, Arnold's barrister friend, or even the dim but irrepressible Theodore Walrond. I give this quotation simply to establish Marguerite's social status as shown by her relation to

Olivia, who would seem to be the daughter of the house. One's whole view of Matt would be altered if it could be proved that at any time in his life he had felt strongly enough to escape the social prejudices which condition the emotional experiences of most men; had, for example, fallen passionately in love with a waitress. So far from transcending these prejudices it will appear that Matt was never quite happy even about Marguerite's social position. When he disparages her it is on moral grounds, but beneath the moral reproof is the implication that she is not quite a lady, and so really anything is to be expected of her.

In "The Terrace at Berne," looking towards the country of his youthful love, and wondering where, after ten years, Marguerite now is, he asks:

"Ah, shall I see thee, while a flush
  Of startled pleasure floods thy brow,
  Quick through the oleanders brush,
  And clap thy hands, and cry: ' 'Tis thou.'

"Or hast thou long since wander'd back,
  Daughter of France! to France, thy home;
  And flitted down the flowery track
  Where feet like thine too lightly come?

"Doth riotous laughter now replace
  Thy smile; and rouge, with stony glare,
  Thy cheek's soft hue; and fluttering lace
  The kerchief that enwound thy hair?"

The argument of this quotation is in the best Victorian tradition. Marguerite, Arnold reflects, though treated as one of the family, was after all a paid dependant. She was therefore not incorporated in the social fabric, only attached to it. Her morals were—ah, well! So very likely she is a prostitute by now.

It is characteristic of Arnold that of his poems to Marguerite only one, "Parting," and that not certainly, deals with their relations in the first year they met. The others are all concerned with the second year, when Marguerite's love was already nearly extinguished.

"Parting" opens with the lines I have already quoted:

> "Ye storm winds of Autumn. . . ."

The metre changes to introduce Marguerite:

> "But on the stairs what voice is this I hear,
> Buoyant as morning, and as morning clear?
> Say, has some wet bird-haunted English lawn
> Lent it the music of its trees at dawn?
> Or was it from some sun-fleck'd mountain brook
> That the sweet voice its upland clearness took?
> But who is this, by the half open'd door,
> Whose figure casts a shadow on the floor?
> The sweet blue eyes—the soft ash-colour'd hair—
> The cheeks that still their gentle paleness wear—
> The lovely lips, with their arch smile that tells
> The unconquer'd joys in which her spirit dwells.

> "Ah! they bend nearer—
> Sweet lips, this way!"

But he draws back:

> "Hark! the wind rushes past us!
> Ah! with that let me go. . . .
> I come, O ye mountains!
> Ye pine-woods, I come!"

He explains his revulsion from her embrace:

> "Forgive me! forgive me!
> Ah! Marguerite, fain
> Would these arms reach to clasp thee!
> But see! 'tis in vain.
>
> "In the void air, towards thee,
> My stretch'd arms are cast;
> But a sea rolls between us—
> Our different past!
>
> "To the lips, ah! of others
> Those lips have been prest,
> And others ere I was,
> Were strain'd to that breast;
>
> "Far, far from each other
> Our spirits have grown;
> And what heart knows another?
> Ah! who knows his own?"

There is no malice or brutality in

> "A sea flows between us—
> Our different past!"

Like Arthur, Arnold tells the woman he loves, "I was ever virgin save for thee," but the woman is not grovelling at his feet, and he does not punctuate the statement with a kick. The remark is forced from him by his distress at the contrast between his own Fox Hovian purity and his beloved's Gallic laxity. It had to be said, but as soon as the words have passed his lips he tries to soften them by generalizing the predicament in which Marguerite and he are placed:

> "Far, far from each other
> Our spirits have grown;
> And what heart knows another?
> Ah, who knows his own?"

To which Marguerite could reasonably have answered that as it appeared they were no worse off than anyone else they might as well, like all the others, make the best of a bad job.

She preferred, however, to say nothing, though she probably understood Arnold's hesitations and disquiet almost from the beginning; but cared for him enough to hope that when he returned after a year's absence he would have shed the prejudices of his misfortunate upbringing.

This is how Arnold describes his return:

> "Again I see my bliss at hand,
> The town, the lake, are here;
> My Marguerite smiles upon the strand,
> Unalter'd with the year.

"I know that graceful figure fair,
That cheek of languid hue;
I know that soft, enkerchief'd hair,
And those sweet eyes of blue.

"Again I spring to make my choice;
Again in tones of ire
I hear a God's tremendous voice:
'Be counselled and retire.' "

A lover who advances with one eye on his line of re-treat is likely to have the retreat he contemplates imposed on him before he feels quite ready for it. This was Arnold's experience.

"Days flew; ah, soon I could discern
A trouble in thine alter'd air;
Thy hand lay languidly in mine,
Thy check was grave, thy speech grew rare.

"I blame thee not!—this heart I know,
To be long loved was never framed;
For something in its depths doth glow
Too strange, too restless, too untamed.

"And women—things that live and move
Mined by the fever of the soul—
They seek to find in those they love
Stern strength, and promise of control.

"They ask not kindness, gentle ways,
These they themselves have tried and known;
They ask a soul which never sways
With the blind gusts that shake their own. . . .

"I too have long'd for trenchant force,
And will like a dividing spear;
Have praised the keen, unscrupulous course,
Which knows no doubt, which feels no fear.

"But in the world I learnt, what there
Thou too wilt surely one day prove,
That will, that energy, though rare,
Are yet far, far less rare than love."

No wonder Marguerite's speech grew rare. The argument developed in this quotation must have seemed so completely beside the point as to make comment impossible. Even to a detached person there is something confusing about Matt in his character of a Fox How Byron, keeping a girl at a distance because of her irregular past and then saying:

(1) That she finds him too strange, too restless, too untamed;

(2) That she doesn't appreciate his kindness and gentle ways; but

(3) That one of these days she *will* appreciate love at its true value.

I have given this quotation at length not only for its bearing on Arnold's love story but also because it illustrates his very imperfect contact with reality. General advisers to the universe are usually at a loss in front of the easiest problems in their own lives.

The simplicity of nature which at times made Arnold absurd preserved him from more than the most superficial symptoms of malice, wounded vanity, or conceit.

None of these qualities is present in the quotations I have made, not even in his speculations on the terrace at Berne, nor in his reference to "our different past," nor in his picture of himself as a misunderstood Byronic hero.

By virtue of this simplicity he often gave perfect expression to the one reality he could always apprehend, his own sense of bewilderment and frustration. In the poem from which I have just been quoting, the verse rises to poetry when his relations with Marguerite are momentarily forgotten:

> "And though we wear our life, alas!
>   Distracted as a homeless wind,
>   In beating where we must not pass,
>   In seeking what we shall not find."

This is Arnold in his deepest and most natural mood, but the optimism which he partly imposed on himself as a duty and partly yielded to as a relief from his melancholy drags him from this level in the next verse.

> "Yet we shall one day gain, life past,
>   Clear prospect o'er our being's whole;
>   Shall see ourselves and learn at last
>   Our true affinities of soul.
>
> "We shall not then deny a course
>   To every thought the mass ignore;
>   We shall not then call hardness force,
>   Nor lightness wisdom any more."

The last verse connects itself with the lines I have already quoted from this poem:

> "I too have long'd for trenchant force,
>   And will like a dividing spear."

His worldliness, on which he prided himself so ingenuously, was one element in the obsession which made him waste so many years in trying to direct mankind along the road to perfection. But it did not sit on him quite naturally. Neither Byron nor Napoleon was the model for him to imitate, a truth which he saw only at rare intervals, and less often as he grew older, and to which he never again gave so clear an expression as in these early lines:

> "We shall not then call hardness force,
>   Nor lightness wisdom any more."

To return to Marguerite. As soon as Matthew realized, or was told, that she no longer loved him, he forgot their different past and the order to retreat sounded by the tremendous voice of a God whose accents were indistinguishable from Dr. Arnold's.

It now seemed to him that his one hope and aim had been to make her happy.

> "We were apart; yet day by day,
>   I bade my heart more constant be,
>   I bade it keep the world away,
>   And grow a home for only thee,
>   Nor fear'd but thy love likewise grew,
>   Like mine, each day, more tried, more true."

(He meant to write "hoped," but "fear'd" slipped
out unconsciously, to express his previous anxiety lest
he should be trapped beyond possibility of escape.)

> "The fault was grave! I might have known.
>   What far too soon, alas! I learn'd.
> The heart can bind itself alone,
>   And faith may oft be unreturn'd.
> Self-sway'd our feelings ebb and swell
> Thou lov'st no more; Farewell! Farewell!

> "Farewell! and thou, thou lonely heart,
>   Which never yet without remorse
> Even for a moment didst depart
>   From thy remote and spherèd course
> To haunt the place where passions reign
> Back to thy solitude again!"

In the last stanza his emotion, disentangling itself from
Marguerite and turning in on himself and his own
sense of isolation, begins to lift the verse to the level
which it reaches in the next poem, "To Marguerite—
Continued."

This poem is perhaps too well known to be quoted
in full, but I give its first and last verse as one of the
finest expressions in Arnold of his central emotion;
though even at this height he has to introduce a God to
check any rebellious movement against the nature of
things.

> "Yes! in the sea of life enisled,
>   With echoing straits between us thrown,
> Dotting the shoreless watery wild,

We mortal millions live *alone*.
The islands feel the enclasping flow
And then their endless bounds they know. . . .

"Who order'd that their longing's fire
Should be, as soon as kindled, cool'd?
Who renders vain their deep desire?
A God, a God their severance ruled!
And bade betwixt their shores to be
The unplumb'd, salt, estranging sea."

"The Forsaken Merman" appeared in 1849, and
"Tristram and Iseult" in 1852. It seems to me probable that they were both written in 1848, though the
third part of Tristram may have been composed later.
Arnold, as has been shown, wrote very indifferently
about Marguerite herself, but as soon as he had left
her, in 1847, I think, and was therefore no longer hampered by the uneasy relations that existed between them,
she became to him a symbol of the happiness he had
missed, quickening his imagination until it attained, in
"The Forsaken Merman," a complete though only
momentary freedom.

"Come away, away children;
Come children, come down!
The hoarse wind blows coldly;
Lights shine in the town.
She will start from her slumber
When gusts shake the door;
She will hear the winds howling,
Will hear the waves roar.
We shall see, while above us

The waves roar and whirl,
A ceiling of amber,
A pavement of pearl,
Singing: 'Here came a mortal
But faithless was she!
And alone dwell for ever
The kings of the sea.'

"But children, at midnight,
When soft the winds blow,
When clear falls the moonlight
When spring-tides are low;
When sweet airs come seaward
From heaths starr'd with broom,
And high rocks throw mildly
On the blanch'd sands a gloom;
Up the still, glistening beaches,
Up the creeks we shall hie,
Over banks of bright seaweed
The ebb-tide leaves dry.
We will gaze from the sand-hills,
At the white, sleeping town;
At the church on the hill-side
And then come back down,
Singing: 'There dwells a loved one,
But cruel is she!
She left lonely for ever
The kings of the sea.' "

"Tristram and Iseult" is less satisfactory as a whole than "The Forsaken Merman," but the second part, where Iseult of Ireland returns to the dying Tristram, gives Arnold scope to express more fully than anywhere else in his work the regret and pathos which were for him the deepest emotions of life and of love.

Before quoting from the second part, I shall follow his own method and set an attempt in the first part to express passion and ecstasy by the side of three supreme examples of love poetry. The contrast will show Arnold's limitations both as a man and as a poet.

Arnold:

> "Let their hands
> Tremble, and their cheeks be flame,
> As they feel the fatal bands
> Of a love they dare not name,
> With a wild delicious pain,
> Twine about their hearts again!
> Let the early summer be
> Once more round them, and the sea
> Blue, and o'er its mirror kind
> Let the breath of the May-wind
> Wandering through their drooping sails,
> Die in the green fields of Wales!
> Let a dream like this restore
> What his eye must see no more!"

Donne—(The Ecstasy):

> "So to engraft our hands, as yet
> Was all the means to make us one,
> And pictures in our eyes to get
> Was all our propagation."

Clerk Saunders:

> "Clerk Saunders and May Margaret
> Walked o'er yon garden green.
> And deep and heavy was the love
> That fell thir twa between."

Othello:

> "If it were now to die,
>   T'were now to be most happy, for I fear
>   My soul hath her content so absolute
>   That not another comfort like to this
>   Succeeds in unknown fate."

The second part opens with the arrival of Iseult of Ireland, as Tristram lies dying. Tristram reproaches her for her long delay in coming to him. She soothes his anger, and he asks if she will now stay with him. She answers:

> "Fear me not, I will be always with thee;
>   I will watch thee, tend thee, soothe thy pain;
>   Sing thee tales of true, long-parted lovers,
>   Join'd at evening of their days again."

He begs her not to speak, lest he should find something altered in her courtly tone. She tells him that love like hers is not altered in the life of courts:

> "Ah, on which, if both our lots were balanced,
>   Was indeed the heaviest burden thrown—
>   Thee, a pining exile in thy forest,
>   Me, a smiling Queen upon my throne?

> "Vain and strange debate, where both have suffer'd,
>   Both have passed a youth consumed and sad,
>   Both have brought their anxious day to evening,
>   And have now short space for being glad!

> "Join'd we are henceforth; nor will thy people,
>   Nor thy younger Iseult take it ill,
>   That a former rival shares her office,
>   When she sees her humbled, pale, and still.

"She will cry: 'Is this the foe I dreaded?
This his idol? this that royal bride?
Ah, an hour of health would purge his eyesight!
Stay, pale Queen! for ever by my side.'

"Hush, no words! That smile, I see, forgives me.
I am now thy nurse, I bid thee sleep.
Close thine eyes—this flooding moonlight blinds them!
Nay, all's well again! thou must not weep."

Tristram's head sinks back. Iseult cries to him to call on God and the Holy Angels, but he hushes her. The time for supplication is past. Then as death touches him, longing and regret are lifted for one moment to passion:

"Now to sail the seas of death and leave thee—
One last kiss upon the living shore!"

Deeper than any of the principles and rules of conduct with which men dignify their respect for society, that is, their fear of their fellow-creatures, lies the instinct to escape from this life into the life revealed, if only for a moment, by any great passion, whether of love or of religion. Death alone can make such an escape permanent, a truth implicit in tragic drama, whose heroes are saved from the return to common existence by the magnanimity of their less fortunate creators. But even for those whom life retakes the memory of this escape mitigates the disgrace of their captivity and the penalties imposed on the recaptured fugitive.

Conversely, those who have seen the way of escape

open and have shrunk from taking it console themselves
in vain with their adherence to principles which they
realize, even if unconsciously, to be based on nothing
deeper or more real than social convenience, or material
interests.

In the lines just quoted from "Tristram and Iseult,"
the "anxious day" and "the youth consumed and sad"
express Arnold's sense of failure in the crisis of his
life. In the dying Tristram he prefigures his own old
age, and the remorse that attends renunciation for renunciation's sake.

The reward of renunciation is some good greater
than the thing renounced. To renounce with no vision
of such a good, from fear or in automatic obedience to
a formula, is to weaken the springs of life, and to diminish the soul's resistance against this world.

This was Arnold's experience. In "Absence," composed after he had left Marguerite, he complains:

> "This is the curse of life! that not
> A nobler, calmer train,
> Of wiser thoughts and feelings blot
> Our passions from our brain.
>
> "But each day brings its petty dust
> Our soon choked souls to fill,
> And we forget because we must
> And not because we will."

The same emotion finds expression in "A Summer
Night." I quote the opening lines, though they do not
bear on the argument of the poem, both for their beauty

and for their revelation of the loneliness and fear which Arnold concealed from the world behind his exaggerated urbanity.

> "In the deserted, moon-blanch'd street,
>   How lonely rings the echo of my feet!
>   Those windows, which I gaze at, frown
>   Silent and white, unopening down,
>   Repellent as the world. . . ."

He remembers suddenly another night:

> "That night was far more fair
>   But the same restless pacings to and fro,
>   And the same vainly throbbing heart was there,
>   And the same bright, calm moon.
>
> "And the calm moonlight seems to say:
>   'Hast thou then still the old unquiet breast,
>   Which neither deadens into rest,
>   Nor ever feels the fiery glow,
>   That whirls the spirit from itself away,
>   But fluctuates to and fro,
>   Never by passion quite possess'd
>   And never quite benumb'd by the world's sway?'"

He then turns to contemplate the two destinies between which he wavers, first picturing the life of the mass of humanity:

> "For most men in a brazen prison live . . .
>   And as, year after year,
>   Fresh products of their barren labour fall
>   From their tired hands, and rest
>   Never yet comes more near,

Gloom settles slowly down over their breast;
And while they try to stem
The waves of mournful thought by which they are prest
Death in their prison reaches them,
Unfreed, having seen nothing, still unblest.

"And the rest, a few,
Escape their prison and depart
On the wide ocean of life anew."

The "freed prisoner" holds on his way confidently
for a time

"And then the tempest strikes him; and between
The lightning-bursts is seen
Only a driving wreck,
And the pale master on his spar-strewn deck
With anguish'd face and flying hair
Grasping the rudder hard,
Still bent to make some port he knows not where,
Still standing for some false, impossible shore,
And sterner comes the roar
Of sea and wind, and through the deepening gloom
Fainter and fainter wreck and helmsman loom,
And he too disappears and comes no more.
Is there no life, but these alone?
Madman or slave, must man be one?"

Arnold's imagination never carried him higher than
in this picture of the freed prisoner wrecked in the
storm; but as a criticism of life, his own test of poetry,
it is false, or at least inadequate. Of those who escape
from the brazen prison, the most are wrecked, but a
few reach the shores of beauty and die in harbour.

Arnold might have been among these, had he not put back to port as soon as the tempest began to threaten.

The poem ends with an invocation of the heavens, who are supposed to exemplify the kind of life possible to mankind.

> "Ye heavens, whose pure dark regions have no sign
> Of languor, though so calm, and though so great,
> Are yet untroubled and unpassionate;
> Who, though so noble, share in the world's toil,
> And though so task'd, keep free from dust and soil!
> I will not say that your mild deeps retain
> A tinge, it may be, of their silent pain,
> Who have long'd deeply once, and long'd in vain.
> But I will rather say that you remain
> A world above man's head, to let him see
> How boundless might his soul's horizons be,
> How vast, yet of what clear transparency!
> How it were good to abide there, and breathe free;
> How fair a lot to fill
> Is left to each man still!"

I shall return later to the argument contained in this passage, the seventh and eighth lines in which almost redeem the false sentiment of the rest. Its unreality is best exposed at the moment by setting Coleridge's lines beside it:

> "O lady, we receive but what we give,
> And in our life alone doth Nature live."

If nature could not supply what his own hesitating grasp had failed to seize from life, still less could the moral precepts imposed on him in his youth. Here, from an imitation Greek chorus, published in the 1849 volume, is a quotation which may fitly round off the story of his love for Marguerite.

"Him then I praise who dares
 To self-selected good
 Prefer obedience to the primal law
 Which consecrates the ties of blood; for those indeed,
 Are to the Gods a care;
 That touches but himself.
 For every day man may be link'd and loosed
 With strangers; but the bond
 Original, deep-inwound
 Of blood, can he not bind,
 Nor, if Fate binds, not bear."

A LTHOUGH we to-day know that Matt dared to prefer to self-selected good obedience to the primal law which consecrates the ties of blood, and dared very little else, the form which his audacity eventually took was for a long time hidden from his friends, and from the inmates of Fox How. Matt, Mrs. Humphry Ward tells us, was the worldling of the family. In the family magazine, compiled at Fox How, his dress and deportment formed a frequent topic for jest; but, as Sergeant Buzfuz noted, "it is ill jesting with an aching heart," and I take it, though I have no direct evidence, that the hearts at Fox How ached frequently during 1846 and 1847. In the latter year he was appointed private secretary to Lord Lansdowne. His years of unrestricted wandering on the Continent were therefore over, and that was something. In Lansdowne House, however, he was in the centre of London society, and his sisters, Mrs. Ward tells us, wondered if he would be "spoiled."

"But how soon," Mrs. Ward cries, "the nascent dread lest their poet should be somehow separated from them by the "great world" passes away from mother and sisters—for ever! With every year of his life Matthew Arnold, beside making the sunshine of his

── MATTHEW ARNOLD
AND MRS. HUMPHRY WARD ──
(From a cartoon by Max Beerbohm)
He was the worldling of the family

own married home, became a more attached, a more
devoted son and brother."

There are two other scraps of evidence, supplied by
Mrs. Ward, from which the anxiety felt about Matt
during the years before his marriage may be inferred.
One of his younger brothers, William Delafield Arnold,
had gone out to India as a subaltern in the Bengal
Native Infantry. His fellow subalterns in particular,
and Anglo-Indian society in general, upset him very
much. "The Alpha and Omega of the whole evil in
Indian Society," he wrote, "is the regarding India as
a super-mine instead of a colony, and ourselves as
Fortune hunters and Pension earners rather than as
emigrants and missionaries." This view, together with
his impressions of his fellow subalterns, he set forth
at length in a novel called "Oakleigh." After his
retirement from the Bengal Native Infantry he devoted himself to educational work, and eventually,
in 1855, became Director of Public Instruction in the
Punjaub. He seems to have been both efficient and con-
scientious, not allowing even the Mutiny to interfere
with his education of the Punjaub.

In one of his letters to his brother Tom, Mrs. Ward's
father, he writes, on hearing of Matt's engagement:
"I own that Matt is one of the very last men in the
world whom I can fancy happily married—or rather
happy in Matrimony [1] . . . dear old Matt."

William's fears about Matt's marriage were obviously

[1] The distinction between "happily married" and "happy in matrimony" is very acute.

connected with the Fox How view of Matt as the worldling of the family; a view also implied in a letter Stanley wrote to Tom two or three years after Matt's marriage. "He is—I must say so, though perhaps I have no right to say so—greatly improved by his marriage—retaining all the genius and nobleness of mind which you remember, with all the lesser faults pruned and softened down."

These "lesser faults," which perhaps included his side-whiskers and a too careful attention to his dress, had already been commented on by Charlotte Brontë, who met Matt in 1850: "His manner displeases by its seeming foppery." She admitted, however, that he had "some genuine intellectual aspirations."

Nothing more forcibly illustrates Matt's inability to refrain, when he saw two stools, from falling between them than the offence he gave Charlotte Brontë as an imitation Bulwer, and the chill he struck to George Sand's warm bosom as an imitation Milton.

So far as he resembled either of these, in their different ways, equally unattractive persons, it is of Milton rather than of Bulwer that he reminds one during his three years at Lansdowne House. Bulwer, in Matt's place, would have spent most of his time searching, in the society of this or that attractive woman, for the True, or, at any rate, for the Beautiful. There is no evidence that Matt's mysterious worldliness took this or any other form. The only picture I have been able to find of him in Lansdowne House is given in a letter he wrote to Tom in New Zealand during the French Revolution of 1848.

"Behind me a most musical clock, marking now 24 minutes past 1 p.m. On my left two great windows looking out on the court in front of the house, through one of which, slightly opened, comes in gushes the soft damp breath, with a tone of spring life in it, which the close of an English February sometimes brings.

"And from the square and the neighbouring streets, through the open door whereat the civil porter moves to and fro, come the sounds of vehicles and men, in all gradations, some from near and some from far, but mellowed by the time they reach this backstanding mansion.

"But above all cries comes one whereat every stone in this and other lordly mansions may totter and quake for fear:

" 'Se—c—ond Edition of the *Morning Herald*. L—a—test news from Paris: Arrival of the King of the French.' "

It is about this date that Arnold's letters, as edited by George Russell, begin. They tell us nothing of Matt's London life or of his relations with Lord Lansdowne and they are completely silent about the events that led up to his engagement, and about his emotions during his engagement. Yet his future wife, Frances Lucy, was the daughter of Sir William Wightman; a match, one would suppose, entirely suitable, and in no way demanding this extreme reticence of treatment.

One pre-nuptial letter to her is, indeed, given, but in a fragmentary form. It deals with Lord John Russell and the Budget. "People," Arnold writes, "speculate on a Clarendon Ministry. If Lord Clarendon comes in Sugden will be Chancellor—not else; he is far too much committed on the Papal aggression question to come in with a Whig or Peelite Ministry—but why do you ask?"

The majority of Matt's letters are to his mother. It is characteristic of him that his style varies very little with his correspondents; but then his correspondents are not of very various types, being usually his mother, one of his sisters, or his wife.

Of Arnold's mother the following quotation, from a letter to Tom Arnold, gives a restful and charming impression; though one feels the wording of the quotation would have been exactly the same if Matt had happened to write Browning's "Men and Women" or Tennyson's "In Memoriam," or, in short, any volume of Victorian poetry, except Swinburne's "Poems and Ballads." "But the little volume of poems! That is indeed a subject of new and very great interest. . . . I am very much mistaken if their power both in thought and execution is not more and more felt and recognized." Of a sense in his family of Arnold himself behind his poetry, I have found no evidence except the following extract from a letter written by his sister Mary, who was already a widow, though only twenty-three:

"His poems seemed to make me know Matt so much

better than I had ever done before." He seemed, she adds later, to have "come face to face with life and asked it, in real earnest, what it means . . . a knowledge of life which was *strangely like experience*, if it was not the thing itself."

In 1848, the year to which the quotations I am about to give belong, Arnold was only twenty-five. His mood, however, was already one of permanent dejection, relief for which he had begun to seek in criticism of the world at large. In March of this year he writes to his mother: "I see a wave of more than American vulgarity, moral, intellectual and social, preparing to break over us. In a few years people will understand better why the French are the most civilized of European peoples, when they see how fictitious our manners and civility have been, how little inbred in the race."

In April he gives a glimpse of the panic caused by the Chartist movement, and an excellent example, in Carlyle's remark, of the danger incurred by a political prophet when he prophesies about events that have not yet occurred.

"He (Carlyle) gives our institutions, as they are called, aristocracy, Church, etc., five years I heard last night. . . .

"The ridiculous terror of the people here is beyond belief. . . . Tell Miss Martineau it is said that Monckton Milnes refused to be sworn in a special constable that he might be free to assume the post of President of the Republic at a moment's notice."

In May he comments on Heine, whom he had not previously read:

"I have just finished a German book I brought with me here: a mixture of poems and travelling journal by Heinrich Heine, the most famous of the young German literary set. He was a good deal of power, though more trick; however, he has thoroughly disgusted me. The Byronism of a German, of a man trying to be gloomy, cynical, impassioned, *moqueur*, etc., all *à la fois*, with their honest bonhommistic language and total want of experience of the kind that Lord Byron, an English peer with access everywhere, possessed, is the most ridiculous thing in the world . . .

I have also been reading "Las Casas," and been penetrated with admiration for Napoleon. . . . His contest with England is in the highest degree tragic. The inability of the English of that time in any way to comprehend him, and yet their triumph over him—and the sense of this contrast in his own mind—there lies the point of the tragedy . . . the number of ideas in his head which 'were not dreamt of in their philosophy.' "

In the first of these quotations, Arnold has already fallen into the trick of generalizing about nations, always a sign in an imaginative writer that he is decaying into a publicist and doctrinaire. While Arnold was praising France as civilized, Flaubert was beginning the portrait of Homais, the typical French provincial.

That only the highest circles of society provide material for gloom and cynicism seems to be the moral of Arnold's remarks on Heine, but I need not linger over this unfortunate quotation, having shown clearly enough, in his relations with Marguerite, that Arnold had a strong infusion of upper-middle class Victorian snobbishness.

Far more significant is the admiration he expresses for Napoleon. Like Bernard Shaw, and other literary sentimentalists, Arnold swallows whole the portrait of Napoleon, the great liberator, composed by Napoleon, during his retirement at Saint Helena. That fleas are good for a dog, and that Napoleon was good for Europe, are propositions which can be accepted without crediting either Napoleon or the flea with any disinterested zeal for human or canine well-being. The greatness of a Lenin, a Cromwell, or a Napoleon does not consist in his ideas, which are those current at the moment, but in his handling of the various difficulties that arise during the convulsions in which from time to time a country or a continent expresses its impatience with the nature of things in general. Lenin in Cromwell's position would have with equal passion called upon the bowels of Christ to judge between him and the Parliament he happened to be throwing out of doors at the moment; and in Lenin's position Napoleon would have had a great deal to say about the dictatorship of the proletariat and nothing at all about the ideas of '89.

What, in terms of concrete reality, Arnold meant by the failure of the English to comprehend Napoleon, it is useless to inquire. Possibly he thought the English Government should have invited Napoleon to bring his troops over from Boulogne on the first fine day.

The return to reality with Arnold is always a return to his own sense of frustration. In January, 1851, six months before his marriage, he wrote to his sister Jane, whom he used to address as "K," a letter remarkable both for its sincerity and its pathos. With the inspectorship of schools to which Lord Lansdowne had appointed him looming ahead, he looks back on his youth and for a moment hangs on the edge of revolt.

"It seems as if we could only acquire any solidity of shape and power of acting by narrowing and narrowing our sphere, and diminishing the number of affections and interests which continually distract us while young, and hold us unfixed and without energy to mark our place in the world; which we thus succeed in marking only by making it a very confined and joyless one. The aimless and unsettled, but also open and liberal state of our youth we *must* perhaps all leave and take refuge in our morality and character; but with most of us it is a melancholy passage from which we emerge shorn of so many beams that we are almost tempted to quarrel with the law of nature which imposes it on us."

Further on in this letter he revives a little. After all, he is writing from Lansdowne House. "I am by nature," he tells his sister, "so very different from you, the worldly element enters so much more largely into my composition." A day or two later he writes to "K" again: "I read Goethe's letters, Bacon, Pindar, Sophocles, Milton, Thomas à Kempis, and Ecclesiasticus, and retire more and more from the modern world, which is all only what has been before and what will be again, and not bracing or edifying in the least."

On this note I shall leave Matt as worldling and turn to his poetry again.

XVII. NATURE

THE bulk of Arnold's poetry, as has been already pointed out, is contained in two volumes, the first, "The Strayed Reveller, etc.," published in 1849, the second, "Empedocles of Etna, and other Poems," published in 1852.

It is safe to infer that nearly all these poems were written during his years at Lansdowne House, between his parting from Marguerite and his marriage in the June of 1851. In 1852 he brought out a new edition, which contained only one poem certainly composed after his marriage—"Sohrab and Rustum." I shall therefore treat the few new poems contained in the 1853 edition as belonging to the same period as the work published in his first two volumes.

A gentle melancholy, as of a lake on a grey windless day, is the prevailing note of Arnold's poetry, when his moralizing bent is not tampering with it.

> "And is the heart of youth so light,
>   Its step so firm, its eyes so bright,
>   Because on its hot brow there blows
>   A wind of promise and repose
>   From the far grave to which it goes?
>   Because it hath the hope to come,
>   One day to harbour in the tomb?
>   Ah, no, the bliss youth dreams is one

For daylight, for the cheerful sun. . . .
It hears a voice within it tell:
'Calm's not life's crown, though calm is well,
'Tis all perhaps which man acquires
But 'tis not what our youth desires!' "

The surface of the lake is ruffled now and then by a gust of impatience or self-distaste. In a sonnet which opens "When I shall be divorced, some ten years hence," the divorce being only, as it turns out, between his present and his future self, he foresees that he will find a thousand virtues in his present youthful disquiet.

"Then I shall praise the heat which then I lack
And call this hurrying fever, generous fire."

But even this heat and hurrying fever are intermittent, and the intervals are filled with blank despondency.

"The thoughts that rain their steady glow
Like stars on life's cold sea,
Which others know or say they know
They never shone for me."

His spring of emotion, as I have shown, was clogged at its source; and his love for Marguerite was not strong enough to force a passage for it through the rubble of his father's moral and religious training. Hence, the peculiar note of his melancholy, as of an exile tamed by his captor, remembering with regret but without rebellion the land to which he once belonged.

"Yet still, from time to time, vague and forlorn,
From the soul's subterranean depth upborne
As from an infinitely distant land,
Come airs and floating echoes, and convey,
A melancholy into all our day."

But he never rested long in such natural and exquisite rendering of his real emotion. His personal attendant, the demon Morality, bequeathed to him by his father as his inseparable companion, enforced on him the necessity of attaching some doleful message of cheer or encouragement to poems, whose sadness, uncorsetted by morality, would have charmed with the charm of all spontaneous expression.

I have already shown, in "A Summer Night," how he tags on to a fine imaginative picture of the two destinies of man an invocation to the heavens to let man see

"How boundless might his soul's horizons be,
How vast, yet of what clear transparency!"

That we get from Nature neither more nor less than what our strength and virtue, if any, entitle us to, and that when life has impoverished us Nature does not replenish our purse with a *pour-boire*, Arnold might have learnt by regarding the long decay of his master Wordsworth. But the habit, instilled into him at Laleham and Rugby, of sheltering behind someone stronger than himself, forced him, in his weaker moods, to convert nature itself into a kind of generalized form of Dr. Arnold; as in the poem "Self-Dependence."

"Weary of myself, and sick of asking
    What I am and what I ought to be,
At this vessel's prow I stand, which bears me
    Forwards, forwards o'er the starlit sea.

"And a look of passionate desire
    O'er the sea and to the stars I send:
Ye who from my childhood up have calm'd me,
    Calm me, ah, compose me to the end!"

Instead of reposing in this image of supernal tranquillity revealed in a starry sky, Arnold lends a voice to the "intense, clear, star-sown vault of heaven," a voice of pained admonishment, strengthened by italics,

"Would'st thou *be* as these are? *Live* as they." How, then, do stars live? Not unlike the best type of Rugby praepostor:

"Unaffrighted by the silence round them,
    Undistracted by the sights they see,
These demand not that the things without them
    Yield them love, amusement, sympathy."

In "The Youth of Nature" he again exalts Nature at the expense of man. The poem opens with a celebration of the places to which Wordsworth had "lent a new life," as he carelessly puts it, forgetting his argument for the moment.

"The pillar still broods o'er the fields
    Which border Ennerdale Lake
    And Egremont sleeps by the sea.
The gleam of the Evening Star

Twinkles on Grasmere no more,
But ruin'd and solemn and grey
The sheepfold of Michael survives,
And, far to the south, the heath,
Still blows in the Quantock coombs,
By the favourite waters of Ruth.
These survive!—yet not without pain,
Pain and dejection to-night!
Can I feel that their poet is gone.
. . . He was a priest to us all
Of the wonder and bloom of the world."

But once more Arnold is unable to rest in the belief that Nature lives only in the interpretation of man. The "voice" is again audible:

"Will ye claim for your great ones the gift
To have render'd the gleam of my skies,
To have echoed the moan of my seas,
Utter'd the voice of my hills?
Race after race, man after man,
Have thought that my secret was theirs,
Have dream'd that I lived but for them,
That they were my glory and joy.
They are dust, they are changed, they are gone!
I remain."

This personifying of Nature as something akin to but greater than man is clearly connected with Arnold's subjection in his early years to his father; and implies the same surrender to an external phenomenon as his glorification of Napoleon. An impression like this cannot be proved, but I am confirmed in it by Arnold's

direct contradiction in one of his sonnets of the attitude
set forth in the quotations just given.

"Know, man hath all which Nature hath, but more,
And in that *more* lie all his hopes of good.
Nature is cruel, man is sick of blood;
Nature is stubborn, man would fain adore;

"Nature is fickle, man hath need of rest;
Nature forgives no debt, and fears no grave;
Man would be mild, and with safe conscience blest,
Man must begin, know this, where Nature ends. . . ."

This self-contradiction constantly occurs in his work,
revealing the struggle between his instinctive sense of
reality and the distorted sense laboriously imposed on
him by his training. The most extraordinary triumph
of the latter is the poem called "Morality," in which
the universal intuitions of mystical experience are completely inverted in order to Victorianize the Absolute.

That Nature is a veil between us and perfection is
in one form or another the common creed of all mystics.
To Blake, Nature was vegetable matter, a gross obstacle
between man and perfection. To Wordsworth, Nature
was a mirror of perfection, clear in childhood but with
each succeeding year more blurred by the mists of common life; or in his own image, perfection is the immortal
sea to whose shores, when Nature is tranquil, the soul
goes back again.

"Hence, in a season of calm weather,
Though inland far we be,

> Our souls have sight of that immortal sea,
> Which brought us hither,
> Can in a moment travel thither,
> And see the children sport upon the shore,
> And hear the mighty waters rolling evermore."

To Blake never, and to Wordsworth only in his un-inspired moments, which, however, were far too frequent, would it have occurred to transport to the regions of ecstasy beyond time and space the moral systems imposed on man as part of the penalty attached to his imprisonment in this world; systems always imperfect and to be regarded at best as ungainly crutches for creatures lamed by the fall from perfection.

Arnold's view is different. In the second stanza of "Morality" he pictures the pains and labour of all achievement.

> "With aching hands and bleeding feet
> We dig and heap, lay stone on stone;
> We bear the burden and the heat
> Of the long day, and wish 'twere done.
> Not till the hours of light return,
> All we have built do we discern."

The work finished, how, he asks, does Nature view

> "thy self control,
> Thy struggling, task'd morality—
> Nature, whose free, light, cheerful air,
> Oft made thee in thy gloom despair?
> ". . . 'Ah, child!' she cries, 'that strife divine,
> Whence was it, for it is not mine?

" 'There is no effort on *my* brow—
    I do not strive, I do not weep;
    I rush with the swift spheres and glow
    In joy, and when I will, I sleep.
    Yet that severe, that earnest air,
    I saw, I felt it once—but where?

" 'I knew not yet the gauge of time,
    Nor wore the manacles of space;
    I felt it in some other clime,
    I saw it in some other place.
    'Twas when the heavenly house I trod,
    And lay upon the breast of God.' "

Nature, that is, appears to Arnold disembarrassed of all limitations, free from effort, and strife, and pain; yet, as she watches the labours of men, their severe and earnest air, reminded of her former estate, when she trod the heavenly house and lying on the breast of God observed in his face the same severe and earnest air.

If I have seemed hitherto to exaggerate the influence of Dr. Arnold on his son, I hope this poem may justify me. Even in the heart of perfection, Matthew sees a magnified Dr. Arnold in charge, disseminating moral influence. Only in a sphere far removed from this Dr. Arnold, in our world, manacled by time and space, can Matthew imagine freedom and joy, which he makes the attributes of Nature; that is of those instincts in himself to which he had never dared to give play, and which, had he given them play, he would have found invested with less freedom and joy than his unconscious self supposed them to possess.

No wonder he could not understand Wordsworth's "Ode," in which perfection is imaged not as a school-master but as an imperial palace, a celestian light, an immortal sea.

XVIII. RESIGNATION

THE repose and consolation which his temperament fitted him to receive from Nature, in those
hours when he put aside the fanciful scheme of morality bequeathed him by his father, are illustrated in
several of his smaller poems, and perhaps with least
admixture of inferior matter in "Kensington Gardens."

> "Sometimes a child will cross the glade
> To take his nurse his broken toy;
> Sometimes a thrush flit overhead
> Deep in her unknown day's employ.
>
> "Here at my feet what wonders pass,
> What endless, active life is here!
> What blowing daisies, fragrant grass!
> An air-stirred forest, fresh, clear."

Even in "Resignation," the elaborate apology for his
lack of life which he addressed to his sister Jane
(Fausta), he refrains from turning Nature into an exemplar of right conduct, as in "Self-Dependence"; or,
as in "Morality," into a force exempt from the limitations that fetter human beings; using her, at the close
of the poem, simply as an image of his own resigned
attitude towards life.

"Yet, Fausta, the mute turf we tread,
The solemn hills around us spread,
This stream which falls incessantly,
The strange-scrawl'd rocks, the lonely sky,
If I might lend their life a voice,
Seem to bear rather than rejoice."

Earlier in the poem, occurs the famous passage in which
he tries to justify his abstention from experience.

"The poet, to whose mighty heart
Heaven doth a quicker pulse impart,
Subdues that energy to scan
Not his own course, but that of man.
Though he move mountains, though his day
Be pass'd on the proud heights of sway,
Though he hath loosed a thousand chains,
Though he hath borne immortal pains,
Action and suffering though he know,
He hath not lived if he live so.
He sees, in some great historied land,
A ruler of the people stand,
Sees his strong thought in fiery flood
Roll through the heaving multitude,
Exults—yet for no moment's space
Envies the all regarded place.
Beautiful eyes meet his—and he
Bears to admire uncravingly.
They pass—he, mingled with the crowd,
Is in their far-off triumphs proud.
From some high station he looks down,
At sunset on a populous town;
Surveys each happy group, which fleets,
Toil ended, through the shining streets,
Each with some errand of its own—

And does not say: *I am alone.*
He sees the gentle stir of birth
When morning purifies the earth. . . .
Lean'd on his gate, he gazes—tears
Are in his eyes, and in his ears
The murmur of a thousand years.
Before him he sees life unroll,
A placid and continuous whole.
That general life, which does not cease,
Whose secret is not joy but peace."

The logic of this apparently lucid argument is confused. It is not the business of the poet to meddle with action, to stand on the proud heights of sway, or send his strong thought through the heaving multitude in fiery flood. That kind of thing he wisely leaves to Mussolini or Horatio Bottomley. The poet feels life not through the collective emotions of a nation or a party, but through contact with individual souls. When, therefore, Arnold pictures the poet declining to mingle in affairs of state, he pictures a platitude; but when he pictures the poet uninflamed by the beauty of women, he is either thinking of Homer and Milton, after they became blind, or he is entirely ignorant of literary history from David and Catullus through Shakespeare and Molière down to Goethe, Burns, Byron, Heine, Shelley and Keats.

In spite of his often reiterated maxim that poetry is a criticism of life, Arnold was only vaguely aware of other men than himself. It would never have occurred to him to test the passage I have quoted by reference to concrete examples; or if it had occurred to him he would have ignored the temptation, for the sake of his own peace of mind, which would have suffered had his argument been proved unsound. The passage therefore lacks solidity, is mere rhetoric, until, leaving the argument behind, he sees himself looking at the world at dawn, when the verse becomes so exquisite that one excuses the poet for generalizing from the tranquillity of the country in the early morning the universal peace of life.

XIX. OBERMANN

ARNOLD wrote two poems on Obermann, with about twenty years' interval between them. The change of tone between the two poems is extremely interesting, but I shall deal with this when I come to "Obermann Once More."

The first "Obermann" has a more sustained sincerity than any other of Arnold's longer poems. The reason for this leads me again into the region of inference.

Except his memorial verses, such as those on Wordsworth, on his father, and on Clough, Arnold never dates his poems. He makes, however, an exception with "Obermann," which is dated November, 1849. This exception might be accounted for on the grounds that this poem was written in commemoration of the author of "Obermann," who, however, had been dead some years; but I doubt if Arnold would have dated it had the poem not been also an elegy on his departed youth.

The poem, he tells us in a note, was conceived, and partly composed, in the valley going down from the foot of the Gemmi Pass towards the Rhone. The scene in which it is laid, however, is the district round Glion, at the eastern end of the Lake of Geneva (Lake Leman).

There is a note on Glion, appended to "Obermann Once More," which leads me to infer that when, in 1846, Arnold left George Sand to go to Switzerland, he went to Thun by way of Lake Geneva and the Simmenthal.

"Probably all who know the Vevey end of the Lake of Geneva," Arnold writes, "will recollect Glion, the mountain village above the Castle of Chillon. Glion now has hotels and *pensions*, and villas; but twenty years ago it was hardly more than the huts of Avant opposite to it—huts through which goes that beautiful path over the Col de Jaman, followed by so many foot travellers on their way from Vevey to the Simmenthal and Thun."

If I am right in supposing that the scene in which "Obermann" is laid was connected in Arnold's memory with the journey that led him to Thun and Marguerite, the mournful sincerity of this poem, written two years after his parting from Marguerite, is explained.

Etienne Pivert de Senancour, the author of "Obermann," and the subject of this poem, is introduced by Arnold to his readers in a note the inaccuracies and suppressions in which are characteristic of Arnold; though I should have been unable to correct them but for information supplied to me by Francis Gribble, a writer equally remarkable for his knowledge of French literature in the eighteenth and nineteenth centuries, and for the ease and wit with which he has communicated this knowledge in his books.

"The author of 'Obermann,' Etienne Pivert de

⁓ OBERMANN ⁓
(Etienne Pivert de Senancour)
He was Arnold's own Discovery

Senancour," Arnold writes, "has little celebrity in
France, his own country; and out of France he is almost
unknown. . . . Senancour was born in 1770. He was
educated for the priesthood, and passed some time in
the seminary of St. Sulpice; broke away from the
Seminary and from France itself, and passed some years
in Switzerland, where he married, returned to France
in middle life, and followed thenceforward the career
of a man of letters, but with hardly any fame or success.
He died an old man in 1846, desiring that on his grave
might be placed these words only: *Éternité deviens
mon asile!*

"The influence of Rousseau, and certain affinities with
more famous and fortunate authors of his own day—
Chateaubriand and Madame de Staël—are everywhere
visible in Senancour. But though, like those eminent
personages, he may be called a sentimental writer, and
though 'Obermann,' a collection of letters from Switzerland treating almost entirely of nature and of the
human soul, may be called a work of sentiment, Senancour has a gravity and severity which distinguish him
from all other writers of the sentimental school. . . .
The stir of all the main forces by which modern life is
and has been impelled, lives in the letters of 'Obermann'; the dissolving agencies of the eighteenth century, the fiery storm of the French Revolution, the first
faint promise and dawn of that new world which our
own world is but now more fully bringing to light—
all these are to be felt, almost to be touched there."

The inaccuracies in this account are less important

than the suppressions. Senancour went to Switzerland
at nineteen, and returning in the following year remained in Paris throughout the Terror. Later he went
back to Switzerland, which he left for the last time,
not in middle life but at thirty-two.

What Arnold either did not know, or did not care to
mention, is the history of Senancour's marriage, which,
as an attempt to put into practice the philosophy expressed in "Obermann," illustrates in its failure the
unsoundness of the philosophy itself, and thus invali-
dates the distinction drawn by Arnold between Senancour and the other sentimentalists of his epoch.

Senancour married a Swiss girl, with whose family
he had stayed at Fribourg and whose mother expected
that her future son-in-law would come into £4,000 a
year. Senancour's family, however, disinherited him
for marrying beneath his rank. Senancour, whose
philosophy was based on a contempt for riches, was not
disturbed by this blow. He removed with his wife to
the Val d' Aosta on the Italian side of the Alps, where
he settled down to contemplate nature unspoilt by man.

His design was to realize in practice the view of life
set forth in his first version of "Obermann," a book
called *"Aldomen, ou le Bonheur dans l'Obscurité."*
Aldomen, like himself, lived in an Alpine retreat, which
he had adorned with a number of rural monuments.
The inscriptions on these monuments enforced simple
truths. Beneath a statue of a woman with a necklace
were the words: "Alas, they are only pearls," and
another monument bore the motto: "I prefer unhesitat-

ingly the ass carrying its burden to the lion seeking whom it may devour." That was Madame Senancour's view, too. She could not be bothered with ravenous lions, but she had a firm belief in burdened asses. An ass without a burden was to her a wasted ass; so Senancour's stay in his Alpine solitude was very short. Returning to Paris, escorted by his wife, he settled down to the pains of hereditary gout, and a long life of drudgery as a publisher's hack. Gout, hack-work, and Madame Senancour explain the inscription he desired to be placed on his tomb, *Éternité deviens mon asile!* though perhaps his meaning would have been even more clearly conveyed had he borrowed the subtitle of his youthful work: *Éternité, ou le Bonheur dans l'Obscurité*.

This was the man whom Arnold ranked with Goethe and Wordsworth as one of the three supreme spiritual guides of the nineteenth century.

The highest praise to which Senancour is entitled is that he had, like Arnold, a gentle and charming gift for expressing the consolation afforded by nature to the lonely and the disillusioned. In his essay on Amiel Arnold gives an extract from Senancour which illustrates his peculiar talent.

"My path lay beside the green waters of the Thiele. . . . I descended a steep bank, and got upon the shore of the lake where its ripple came up and expired. The air was calm; everyone was at rest; I remained there for hours. Towards morning the moon shed over the earth and waters the ineffable melancholy of her last gleams. Nature seems unspeakably grand, when, plunged in a long reverie, one hears the rippling of the waters upon a solitary strand, in the calm of a night still enkindled and luminous with the setting moon."

The "Stanzas in Memory of the Author of Obermann," to give the poem its full title, open with a picture of the Gemmi Pass, which leads from the Rhone Valley to the Bernese Oberland.

> "In front the awful Alpine track
> Crawls up its rocky stair;
> The Autumn storm-winds drive the rack
> Close o'er it in the air."

"Obermann," whom he had read in his earlier visits to Switzerland, revives in Arnold's memory.

> "I turn thy leaves! I feel their breath
> Once more upon me roll;
> That air of languor, cold, and death
> Which brooded o'er thy soul. . . .

> "A fever in these pages burns
> Beneath the calm they feign;
> A wounded human spirit turns,
> Here, on its bed of pain."

Beyond the mountain air which blows through its pages, beneath the murmur of dark-boughed pines, the bells of the cattle, the hum of bees and sound of lonely torrents, Arnold hears:

> "I know what ground—tone
> Of human agony.

> "Immovable thou sittest, still
> As death, composed to bear!
> Thy head is clear, thy feeling chill,
> And icy thy despair."

Why does Arnold, who has previously pictured Obermann as a wounded spirit on a bed of pain now present him as immovable, still as death? Between these two pictures comes the classification of Obermann with Wordsworth and with Goethe, "the strong much-toiling sage"; and it is no doubt to justify this extraordinary comparison that Arnold elevates Obermann to the dignity of a Sphinx. But Obermann soon comes to life again in the exquisite stanzas in which the memory of Marguerite interpenetrates, I think, the vision of the incomparable lake along whose shores Arnold had passed to meet her.

> "How often, where the slopes are green
> On Jaman, hast thou sate
> By some high chalet-door, and seen
> The summer-day grow late,
>
> "And darkness steal o'er the wet grass
> With the pale crocus starr'd,
> And reach that glimmering sheet of glass
> Beneath the piny sward,
>
> "Lake Leman's waters, far below!
> And watch'd the rosy light
> Fade from the distant peaks of snow;
> And on the air of night

"Heard accents of the eternal tongue
Through the pine branches play.
Listen'd, and felt thyself grow young!
Listen'd and wept—Away!

"Away the dreams that but deceive
And thou, sad guide, adieu!
I go, fate drives me; but I leave
Half of my life with you."

These lines are Arnold's farewell to what in the letter to his sister he calls "the aimless and unsettled, but also open and liberal state of our youth." "We," he continues:

"We in some unknown Power's employ
Move in a rigorous line;
Can neither, when we will, enjoy,
Nor, when we will, resign.

"I in the world must live; but thou,
Thou melancholy shade!
Wilt not, if thou canst see me now,
Condemn me nor upbraid."

In this appeal to Obermann, he is excusing himself to his own youth, with its dream of a life spent neither in the world, nor out of it, a life of love without its pains, and meditation without its ennui, and experience without its disillusionment. It is to his youth, awakened from this dream, that the last verse is addressed:

"Farewell! under the sky we part
In this stern Alpine dell!
O unstrung will! O broken heart!
A last, a last farewell!"

IF the entry on "Obermann" is disproportionately long, it is through sympathy with Arnold's own lingering near his vanished youth. It is time, however, to descend into the plain.

There is a poem, published in the 1852 volume, called "Consolation." The poet shows us himself hemmed round everywhere by "smoky dwarf houses," mist clogs the sunshine, a vague dejection weighs down his soul. Yet, he reflects, while he languishes, the sun, far hence in Asia, shines bright on the smooth convent roofs and gilt terraces of holy Lhassa. By the yellow Tiber, in their cool gallery, grey time-worn marbles hold the pure Muses, and they still look fair, etc., etc.

The consolation afforded by distance, in space or in time, needs to be sparingly indulged in, and always with an alert sense that the delight felt is caused not by the objects as they really are, but as they appear at a distance. Arnold, owing to his growing distaste for the reality about him, consoled himself in this way far too frequently, and without the necessary qualification, thus further weakening his sense of the actual. It is one of the chief influences in his attachment to the classics.

"Who prop, thou ask'st in these bad days, my mind?" he says to a friend in a well-known sonnet, and gives three names, Homer, Epictetus, and Sophocles.

I am glad to see that Professor Saintsbury, a lover of the classics and in all things literary and political a Tory of the most extreme type, is yet rendered uneasy by this sonnet.

"One may less admire," he says, "despite its famous and often-quoted line.

'Who saw life steadily, and saw it whole'

the sonnet 'To a Friend,' praising Homer, and Epictetus and Sophocles, for it seems to some to have a snatch of priggishness."

The priggishness seems to be incidental, a by-product of a more serious malady. An Englishman living in the middle of the nineteenth century who really felt the greatness of the ancients would inevitably feel still more intimately the greatness of a fellow countryman, Shakespeare or Wordsworth. We arrive at what is permanent and universal in a foreign writer through his affinity to the writers of our own blood.

It is, therefore, at least as much their remoteness from his own life, as their relevance to it, which attached Arnold to the classics; a point to which I shall return later.

This incapacity to see the past unfalsified by distance becomes still more intense when he passes from Greek and Latin literature to the Bible. In a poem called "The Future," he asks:

"What girl
Now reads in her bosom as clear
As Rebekah read when she sate

At eve by the palm-shaded well?
Who guards in her breast
As deep, as pellucid a spring
Of feeling, as tranquil, as sure?

"What bard,
At the height of his vision, can deem
Of God, of the world, of the soul,
With a plainness as near,
As flashing as Moses felt
When he lay in the night by his flock
In the starlit Arabian waste?
Can rise and obey,
The beck of the Spirit like him?"

As Arnold spent several years of his life in affirming that the Bible was humanity's supreme manual of morality touched by emotion, it will be as well to examine the virtue inherent in the two Bible characters, Rebekah and Moses, elevated, in the quotation just given, above all modern examples. Such an examination will show, among other things, how far Arnold saw "the object as in itself it really is."

Abraham sent the eldest servant of his house to find a wife for his son Isaac among the women of Abraham's native country. The servant took ten of Abraham's camels, and travelled with them to Nahor in Mesopotamia. Arriving in the evening, he dismounted outside the city by a well. Rebekah, "a damsel very fair to look upon, a virgin," approached the well with her pitcher. The servant begged for water, which she gave him and his camels. When the camels had quenched

their thirst, the servant presented Rebekah with a
golden earring, and two golden bracelets. Rebekah then
invited the servant to return to her father's house, with
his camels, and lodge there for the night. Laban,
Rebekah's brother, had meanwhile come to the well,
and, "when he saw the earring and bracelets upon his
sister's hands," he supported his sister's invitation.
"Come in, thou blessed of the Lord; wherefore stand-
est thou without?"

The servant returned with Laban and Rebekah, and,
after attending to his camels and washing his feet, gave
an account of himself and his mission, dwelling at some
length on the wealth of his master Abraham, and pro-
posing a marriage between Rebekah and Isaac. Laban
and his father Bethuel answered: "The thing proceed-
eth from the Lord."

Rebekah, who had been present during these negotia-
tions, was asked by her mother and Laban if she was
prepared to leave her home the following morning, in
order to marry Isaac. She replied, "I will go."

The two sons of Rebekah by her marriage with Isaac
were Jacob and Esau. Esau was Isaac's favourite, Jacob
Rebekah's.

One day, when Isaac was near death, he asked Esau
to go hunting and bring him back some venison, "such
as I love, that my soul may bless thee before I die."
Rebekah overheard this injunction, dressed Jacob in
Esau's clothes, put the skins of kids on his hands and
the smooth of his neck, so as to imitate the hairiness of
his brother Esau, and sent him to Isaac with a dish of

kid's flesh. Isaac, whose eyesight had nearly gone, was deceived by the roughness of Jacob's hands and gave him the blessing intended for Esau; thus, by the custom of that tribe, making Jacob Esau's overlord.

Such is the history of Rebekah, of whom Arnold asks whether any modern woman guards in her breast as deep a spring of feeling, as pellucid, as tranquil, as sure.

The oppression of the Hebrews by the Egyptians was the dominant theme of Moses' thoughts in his early years; and as soon as he came to manhood he killed an Egyptian who was striking a fellow Hebrew, and fled the country. In the land of Midian, as he kept the flocks of his father-in-law Jethro, Moses brooded over the Egyptian oppression, until one night the conviction that he had been chosen to lead the children of Israel out of Egypt into the land inhabited, for the time being, by the Canaanites, Hittites, Amorites and other tribes, came to him in the form of a communication from God.

This is how God spoke to Moses. "And I am sure that the king of Egypt will not let you go, no, not by a mighty hand. And I will stretch out my hand, and smite Egypt with all my wonders which I will do in the midst thereof: and after that he will let you go. And I will give his people (the Hebrews) favour in the sight of the Egyptians: and it shall come to pass, that, when ye go, ye shall not go empty: But every woman shall borrow of her neighbour, and of her that sojourneth in her house, jewels of silver, and jewels of gold, and raiment: and ye shall put them upon your daughters; and ye shall spoil the Egyptians."

It was in this form that the work he was destined to achieve presented itself to Moses in exile in Midian. It was a form appropriate to the matter it dealt with; but it is difficult to see what effective answer, other than a sudden and fatal blow, Arnold could have made to anyone who had replied to:

> "What bard
>   At the height of his vision, can deem
>   Of God, of the world, of the soul,
>   With a plainness as near,
>   As flashing as Moses felt . . . ?"

with "Every woman shall borrow of her neighbour, and of her that sojourneth in her house, jewels of silver, and jewels of gold, and raiment: and ye shall put them upon your daughters; and ye shall spoil the Egyptians."

THE word "prop" was well chosen by Arnold in the line "Who prop, thou ask'st, in these bad days my mind?" For reasons already sufficiently gone into, his mind could not stand up securely without a support of some kind, now the voice of Nature drawing attention to itself as an exemplar of right conduct, now the absolute embodied in Dr. Arnold, and now the contemplation of spiritual insight in a Moses or primal innocence in a Rebekah.

As usual with Arnold, his own work supplies in one place the correction of a false attitude struck in another. In "Empedocles on Etna," published in 1852, he writes:

> "Once read thy own breast right,
>   And thou hast done with fears;
> Man gets no other light,
>   Search he a thousand years."

But in the following year he withdrew this volume from circulation, and issued a volume containing most of the poems in the first two volumes, but with "Empedocles" omitted, and with some new poems, including "Sohrab and Rustum," added. This volume was introduced by his first important piece of literary criticism, a preface in which he takes his omission of "Empedocles" as a text for a discussion on the true subject-matter of poetry.

He explains his dissatisfaction with "Empedocles" in the following passage. "What, then, are the situations, from the representation of which, though accurate, no poetical enjoyment can be derived? They are those in which the suffering finds no vent in action; in which a continuous state of mental distress is prolonged, unrelieved by incident, hope, or resistance; in which there is everything to be endured, nothing to be done. In such situations there is inevitably something morbid, in the description of them something monotonous. When they occur in actual life, they are painful, not tragic; the representation of them in poetry is painful also."

One of the decisive moments in Arnold's life, both as a man and as a poet, was when he ran away from "Empedocles" and took refuge in "Sohrab and Rustum." It is true that, as a whole, "Empedocles" is a failure, but Arnold does not diagnose the cause of the failure rightly. "The suffering," he writes, "finds no vent in action . . . a continuous state of mental distress is prolonged, unrelieved by incident, hope, or resistance . . . there is everything to be endured, nothing to be done."

The extraordinary inference to be drawn from this passage is that unless suffering issues in action it is not a fit theme for poetry; "no poetical enjoyment can be derived" from it. There is no action in lyrical poetry;

therefore all lyrics inspired by suffering are ruled out as poetry by this formula of Arnold's.

Naturally, Arnold would have questioned this inference; he might have drawn attention to the phrase "a continuous state of mental distress," and argued that the short compass of most lyrics excludes the effects of monotony and depression. He might, of course, have thought of some better answer, but this is the best I can provide him with, and it is inadequate. One of the greatest lyrics in English is Wordsworth's "Affliction of Margaret," which deals from beginning to end with a state of mental distress, as continuous and as unrelieved by incident, hope, or resistance, as any state of human emotion could possibly be. Yet the poem, so far from being either morbid or monotonous, is invigorating and thrilling in the highest degree, and reaches its most exalted pitch in its most despairing stanza.

> "My apprehensions come in crowds,
> I dread the rustling of the grass,
> The very shadows of the clouds
> Have power to shake me as they pass.
> I question things and cannot find
> One that will answer to my mind,
> And all the world appears unkind."

This single example is sufficient to prove that to raise the theme he is dealing with, whether one of passive suffering or of heroic action, out of ordinary life, and to renew it in the world of his own imagination, is the sole condition the poet must comply with in order to provide his readers with poetical enjoyment.

Arnold had neither the native force nor the acquired experience needed to renew his themes in the world of his imagination. That, and not any imperfection in the subject itself, is the reason why "Empedocles" is a failure. The subject-matter of "Empedocles on Etna" is Arnold's own melancholy outlook, as illustrated in the letters and personal lyrics already quoted from. But the various obligations imposed on him by his upbringing, to be hopeful, to be moral, to help others to be moral, etc., fettered his imaginative freedom. He lacked the courage to paint real despair. Empedocles, the Sicilian philosopher, who grumbles about life on the summit of Mount Etna, until the numbing cloud suddenly mounts off his soul, and to prevent its settling again he plunges into the crater, is a diluted Byronic figure. This is how he appears to Callicles, the young harp player.

> "And I could watch him with his proud sad face,
>   His flowing locks and gold-encircled brow,
>   And kingly gait, for ever."

And Pausanias is much concerned because

> "He has laid the use of music by
>   And all which might relax his settled gloom."

A figure of this order belongs not to dramatic poetry but to a Bulwer Lytton romance; nor is he made any more real by the many fine emotional and meditative passages which Arnold puts in his mouth. The poem is a failure not through lack of action, but because

Arnold had never immersed himself in life, the probation required of those who desire to recreate the world imaginatively.

When Arnold realized that "Empedocles" was a failure, instead of "reading his own breast right," and seeing the cause of the failure in his own wavering hold on life, he looked round for a prop, and found it in the maxim, to illustrate which he wrote "Sohrab and Rustum," that "all depends on the subject." In other words, the theme is to lift the poet, not the poet the theme. "The eternal objects of poetry, among all nations, and at all times," Arnold says, in the preface of 1853, "are actions; human actions; possessing an inherent interest in themselves, and which are to be communicated in an interesting manner by the art of the Poet."

Anyone unacquainted with Arnold's personal history, but aware of his high reputation as a critic, might waste many hours trying to make sense of this definition. It excludes, in the first place, all lyrical poetry, and all impassioned meditation, from Ecclesiastes to Goethe and Wordsworth. But it is no less bad on the positive side than on the negative side. It states that an action is inherently interesting, interesting in itself, that is, apart from its relation to the experience of the poet who treats it. Achilles dragging Hector round the walls of Troy is interesting, Othello strangling his wife is interesting; therefore Shakespeare, at the particular stage of emotion and experience when he chose the theme of

Othello, might, according to Arnold, have equally well chosen the theme of Achilles and Hector.

The only value of this definition is in the additional proof it supplies of Arnold's dependence on external support of one kind or another. To the fortifying morality of Nature he now adds "noble and significant" actions, but

> "O Matthew, we receive but what we give,
> And in our life alone do actions live."

The great actions with which the poet is to occupy himself, Arnold continues, should be placed in some past setting. This was the practice of the Greeks, and the Greeks, he says, understood the all-importance of the subject far better than the moderns; and from this superiority in subject-matter was derived the greater interest of their personages.

"Achilles, Prometheus, Clytemnestra, Dido—what modern poem presents personages as interesting, even to us moderns, as these personages of an 'exhausted past?'"

Against Achilles, Prometheus, Clytemnestra and Dido, he sets Hermann and Dorothea, Childe Harold, Jocelyn, and the characters in Wordsworth's "Excursion"; and decides, "fearlessly," in favour of the ancients.

I need not waste much time on Arnold's notion of more or less interesting dramatic personages. Had he been genuinely interested in characterization, he would not have pitted Wordsworth and Lamartine, Byron and Goethe (not as the creator of Gretchen and Mephistopheles but of Hermann and Dorothea) against the ancients. He would have chosen Falstaff, Hamlet, and Cleopatra from Shakespeare, and for his other examples would have gone to the modern development of the drama, the novel, and found in Cervantes, Fielding, and Sterne character-drawing far more profound and complex than any Greek or Roman achieved. The greatness of Homer, Æschylus, and Virgil does not reside in their portraits of men and women. The real advantage of placing a theme in a distant setting was not clear to Arnold, and he therefore supports it with the wrong argument. The Victorian belief that human nature had been transformed by the mechanical improvements of that age was expressed, in terms of literary criticism, in the theory the retort to which I have just quoted: "the Poet must leave the exhausted Past and draw his subjects from matters of present import." It is no answer to this to affirm that Achilles is more interesting, even to us moderns, than Childe Harold, or Dido than Dorothea. That is a matter of opinion, and the wisest opinion would probably be that all four are about equally uninteresting.

The advantage to a writer of setting his theme in a past age, or in a foreign country, is simply that he can see it better at a distance, and treat it more freely. Arnold, it is true, seems aware of this in one passage, where he writes: "The Greeks felt no doubt with their exquisite sagacity that an action of present times was too near them, too much mixed up with what was accidental and passing, to form a sufficiently good, self-detached, and self-subsistent object for a tragic poem." But his hold on this truth is very insecure. Just previously he had written: "The date of an action signified nothing: the action itself, its selection and construction, this is what is all-important."

His preference for a theme in a distant setting, therefore, is at bottom emotional, not æsthetic; and springs from his distaste for his own age, which he condemns in this preface as "an age wanting in moral grandeur and spiritual health."

It was not in this depressed spirit that Shakespeare turned for his themes from the England of his day to Italy, Denmark, and ancient Rome; or was it by pure chance. Shakespeare's Romans, Danes and Italians are not, as is often said, merely disguised Elizabethans. By transporting his Elizabethans to other times and countries, Shakespeare purged them of most of their local and temporal peculiarities. They are five parts men and one part Elizabethan. Had he set his plays in contemporary England, the Elizabethan element might have outweighed the universal. With Shakespeare, in fact, one may assume this must have been so, for working at the rate he did he could hardly have attained complete imaginative freedom unless he had placed his theme, before he began on it, at a safe distance. Had he had the leisure of Flaubert or Tolstoi he might have treated contemporary themes with as much detachment as themes removed from him in space or time.

In short, the only concern of a writer, once he has chosen his theme, is that there should be a certain distance between it and himself. If the theme is ancient, it is already removed from the writer. If it is contemporary it is the writer who must remove himself from the theme. That the separation, in the latter instance, is ever quite as complete as in the former is, perhaps, doubtful.

As to the choice of a theme, a part of his argument which throughout this preface Arnold mixes up with the setting of the theme, the writer alone can determine what theme stands in vital relation to his own experience, and he is not likely to find this theme in a gallery filled with plaster casts of ancient heroes. But to discuss the choice of themes at all is a waste of time, for a theme can hardly be said to exist until it has been treated.

In his rejection of "Empedocles," and in this busying of himself with action, Arnold was escaping from life under the pretence of entering more deeply into it. His way into life lay through the despair of Empedocles, not through the sword-play of Sohrab and Rustum.

XXII. THE NARRATIVE POEMS

OF the ballads and narrative or quasi-narrative poems written by Arnold, the merit is in each instance in inverse proportion to the heroic quality of the theme. They appear to have been composed expressly to disprove every position that Arnold attempts to establish in the preface I have just discussed.

In the finest of them, "The Forsaken Merman," the action is as follows: Margaret, the merman's wife, tells him she must go to the upper world, for it is Easter Day, and she must pray with her kinsfolk "in the little grey church on the shore." The Merman allows her to go, but she does not come back; and at last the Merman takes his children and together they go to look for her. They approach the church, and climbing on to the grave-stones look through the leaded panes. The Merman sees Margaret by a pillar, and whispers to her to come back, but she keeps her eyes fixed on the prayer book, and the Merman and the children go down to the sea again.

That is all the action, but more is not needed. The theme is so suited to Arnold's experience and temperament that for once, rising above direct self-expression, he finds a perfect imaginative form for his emotion.

In "Tristram and Iseult" it is difficult to discover

any action at all, beyond the return of Iseult of Ireland to the dying Tristram. The emotion of the poem inheres not in its action but in the lovers' retrospect over their wasted lives.

In the "Church of Brou" the action is set forth in the first part of the poem, entitled "The Castle." The theme is the killing of the Duke of Savoy by a wild boar.

> "Pale and breathless came the hunters;
>   On the turf lies dead the boar,
>   God! the Duke lies stretch'd beside him,
>   Senseless, weltering in his gore."

The Duke's body is borne back to the castle, and his young wife, the Duchess Marguerite, till that hour "clothed in smiles," never smiles again. Leaving her castle, she goes up into the mountains, to complete the building of an unfinished church, the Church of Brou.

> "There she sate, and watch'd the builders,
>   Till the church was roof'd and done,
>   Last of all the builders rear'd her
>   In the nave a tomb of stone."

Two forms are sculptured on the tomb, the Duke in helm and armour, the Duchess in her veil.

> "Round the tomb the carved stone fretwork
>   Was at Easter-tide put on.
>   Then the Duchess closed her labours,
>   And she died at the St. John."

The second part of the poem is called "The Church":

> "On Sundays at the matin-chime,
>   The Alpine peasants, two and three,
>   Climb up here to pray;
>   Burghers and dames, at summer's prime,
>   Ride out to church from Chambery,
>   Dight with mantles gay,
>   But else it is a lonely time
>   Round the Church of Brou."

The third part is "The Tomb."

In the first part, "The Castle," where there is plenty of action, the verse is pure doggerel. In the second part, "The Church," where there is still some stir of life, the verse, though no longer doggerel, is uninspired. In "The Tomb," at a safe remove from all action, alone with the dead Duke and Duchess, Arnold pours himself out in a magnificent strain of exaltation in no way connected with the story set forth earlier in the poem.

> "So rest, for ever rest, O princely Pair!
>   In your high church, 'mid the still mountain air,
>   Where horn and hound, and vassals never come,
>   Only the blessed saints are smiling dumb,
>   From the rich painted windows of the nave,
>   On aisle, and transept, and your marble grave."

Or, if they are to wake let it be

> "On autumn nights, when rain
>   Doth rustlingly above your heads complain,

On the smooth leaden roof, and on the walls,
Shedding her pensive light at intervals
The moon through the clere-story windows shines,
And the wind washes through the mountain pines.
Then, gazing up 'mid the dim pillars high,
The foliaged marble forest where ye lie,
'Hush,' ye will say, 'it is eternity!
This is the glimmering verge of heaven, and these
The columns of the heavenly Palaces!'
And in the sweeping of the wind, your ear
The passage of the Angel's wings will hear,
And in the lichen-crusted leads above,
The rustle of the eternal rain of love."

Now for the two narrative poems, "Sohrab and
Rustum," and "Balder Dead," written after the preface of 1853, and in direct exemplification of the
theories there set forth. But before examining these
two narratives, I must glance at "The Sick King in
Bokhara," an earlier and therefore less deliberate and
self-conscious attempt to waylay inspiration with an action, a human action.

The story, which has an Oriental setting, is of a man
who, suffering from fever during a drought, found a
little pool, filled his pitcher, and took it home. During
the night, "which was with wind and burning dust,"
he got up and went to the pitcher, which his brethren
had found and the contents of which they and his
mother had drunk up. The man "brake forth and
cursed" his brethren and his mother. The next day he
set himself in the path of the King, who was himself in
poor health, and tried to confess his crime in cursing

his mother and his brethren. The King ordered his guard to prick the man from his path with their spears. On the following day the man again tried to confess himself to the King, and was again driven away. On the third day the man once more presented himself before the King, who at last heard him and consented that he should be tried for his offence. The priests, in accordance with the law, sentenced him to be stoned to death. The King, reluctant to enforce this verdict, took a stone and cast it softly, hoping that the man would be satisfied with this nominal execution of the verdict,

> "but the man
> With a great joy upon his face,
> Kneel'd down, and cried not, neither ran.

> "So they, whose lot it was, cast stones,
>   That they flew thick, and bruised him sore,
> But he praised Allah with loud voice,
>   And remain'd kneeling as before."

The King was grieved by his death, to the vexation of his Vizier, who, in a long speech, set forth that there were a great many inevitable causes for sorrow in the world.

> "Fathers we *must* have, wife and child,
>   And grievous is the grief for these."

Why then trouble oneself over "this dead dog?"

The King replies, in a speech of slightly greater length, in which he argues that his wealth and luxury and position have not brought him happiness.

"And I have meat and drink at will,
And rooms of treasure, not a few,
But I am sick, nor heed I these;
And what I would I cannot do."

But one thing he can do, and that is bury "in a fretted brick-work tomb this man my pity could not save."

"Bring water, nard, and linen rolls!
Wash off all blood, set smooth each limb!
Then say: 'He was not wholly vile,
Because a king shall bury him'!"

The theme of this poem, so far as it can be disentangled from the diffuse narrative in which Arnold has embedded it, is the expiation of a guilty soul by a self-chosen death. Dostoieffsky has treated a similar theme in "Crime and Punishment." The final scene in that novel is by no means free from hysteria and false sentiment, but Dostoieffsky does not show us the Czar dispatching Raskolnikoff to Siberia with a guard of honour, and then reflecting that Raskolnikoff has, after all, emerged from the whole affair with some distinction. This effect was reserved for Arnold, and was the due penalty of holding that all depends on the subject, and nothing on the imaginative grasp of the subject by the person treating it.

In May, 1853, Arnold wrote to his mother: "All my spare time has been spent on a poem ('Sohrab and Rustum') which I have just finished, and which I think by far the best thing I have yet done . . . the story is a very noble and excellent one."

The story, which Arnold took from Sir Malcolm's "History of Persia," is of a single combat in front of the Persian and Tartar armies, between a father and a son, who discover their relationship only after the son has been mortally wounded.

A better theme as a vehicle for his own experience Arnold could not have found; but throughout the interminable poem there is hardly a hint of any relation between Thomas and Matthew Arnold on the one hand, and Rustum and Sohrab on the other. Even in the death of Sohrab the emotional pressure behind the verse seems to me, though I am not quite sure, too weak to suggest any conscious or unconscious recognition on Arnold's part of the likeness between his fate and Sohrab's.

> "His limbs grew slack; motionless, white, he lay—
> White, with eyes closed; only when heavy gasps,
> Deep heavy gasps quivering through all his frame,
> Convulsed him back to life, he open'd them,
> And fix'd them feebly on his father's face;
> Till now all strength was ebb'd, and from his limbs
> Unwillingly the spirit fled away,
> Regretting the warm mansion which it left,
> And youth, and bloom, and this delightful world."

Apart from this passage, in which a faint relation between his own experience and his theme is perhaps discernible, the poem is remarkable for nothing but the elaborate laying-on of local colour and the long-drawn-out similes, smacking or intended to smack of

the vital simplicities of primitive life. When Sohrab
and Rustum rush at one another, "a din

> "Rose, such as that the sinewy woodcutters
> Make often in the forest's heart at morn,
> Of hewing axes, crashing trees . . ."

When Rustum, still ignorant that he has been fighting
with his son, stands over the dying Sohrab, Arnold
compares him to a hunter in the spring "who hath
found

> "A breeding eagle sitting on her nest,
> Upon the craggy isle of a hill-lake,
> And pierced her with an arrow as she rose,
> And follow'd her to find her where she fell
> Far off; anon her mate comes winging back
> From hunting, and a great way off descries
> His huddling young left sole; at that, he checks
> His pinion, and with short uneasy sweeps
> Circles above his eyry, with loud screams . . ."

and so on for eight more lines.

On re-examining this simile, I find that it is to the
breeding eagle's mate, not to the hunter, that Rustum
is compared; but it really doesn't matter.

As to local colour, we learn that the Tartars of Fer-
ghana have scanty beards and close-set skull-caps, that
the Tartars of the Oxus are large men on large steeds,
and ferment the milk of mares, a practice unknown to
"the more temperate Toorkmuns of the south," that
Peran-Wisa, the Tartar chieftain, carried a ruler's staff

in his right hand, but no sword, and wore a sheepskin cap, black, glossy, curl'd, the fleece of Kara-Kul; and so on.

"What, then," Arnold asks in the preface of 1853, "are the situations, from the representation of which, though accurate, no poetical enjoyment can be derived?"

Were Arnold alive, I should lead him discreetly apart, and tell him that the answer to this question would probably occur to him after a re-reading of "Sohrab and Rustum."

"Balder Dead" was published two years after "Sohrab and Rustum." The subject is taken from Norse mythology. This attempt of Arnold's to revitalize himself by contact with the primeval is an even more complete failure than his excursion on the same errand into the rude life of the Orient. But I would not linger on Arnold as a poetic Voronoff, submitting himself to the monkey-gland treatment of pseudo-Homeric narrative. I think I have said all that is necessary on this matter; and, besides, I have never been able to get through "Balder Dead." I gave it up half-way through and turned to the close. Read without its context, there is an obscure pathos in the final line:

"At last he sigh'd, and set forth back to Heaven."

Poor chap!

XXIII. RECONCILIATIONS

THE range of Arnold's talent, and the ill effects that attended his ventures outside that range, have now, I hope, been made clear. The themes that suited his talent were loss and regret, and the sense of frustration, and Nature in its gentler aspects, as the mirror of these emotions. His attempts to widen and strengthen the narrow foundations on which he built were all failures. He could manage neither action nor human character; his contact with these was not spontaneous, but imposed on him by a theory, the theory itself being invented as a means of escape from himself. The various forms in which this desire for escape embodied itself have already been given: Nature as Conduct, Dr. Arnold as the Absolute, Moses, Rebekah, Sohrab and Rustum, Balder. Eventually all these forms were to dissolve into each other, from this dissolution after a certain interval emerging Matthew Arnold, prophet of a new world and adviser to mankind how to achieve that fullness of life to which he had himself failed to attain.

Hope, encouragement, and reconciliation, all artificially induced, appeared early in Arnold's poetry. One example has already been quoted, at the close of "A Summer Night":

> "How fair a lot to fill
> Is left to each man still!"

Even in the poem which deals with Moses and Rebekah a note of optimism is struck faintly:

> "Haply, the river of Time . . .
> May acquire, if not the calm
> Of its early mountainous shore,
> Yet a solemn peace of its own."

The injunction, too, to behave like the stars, connects itself with the meliorist strain in Arnold.

I shall try to show later on that a concern with the perfectibility of mankind is always a symptom of thwarted or perverted development. Even in so comparatively slight a nature as Arnold, this can be seen in the difference in depth and intensity between the expression of what he thought he ought to feel and what he really felt. Contrast, for example,

> "But I will rather say that you remain
> A world above man's head, to let him see
> How boundless might his soul's horizons be,
> How vast, yet of what clear transparency!"

with these lines from an early sonnet,

> "This vale, this earth, whereon we dream,
> Is on all sides o'ershadowed by the high
> Uno'erleap'd Mountains of Necessity,
> Sparing us narrower margin than we deem."

A false moral tendency in a writer always has its

æsthetic counterpart. The strain in Arnold, which in the sphere of conduct showed itself as meliorism, reveals itself also in the reconciling close which, as it refused to issue naturally out of the theme, he tacked on forcibly to several of his more important poems.

There is, for example, the ending to "Sohrab and Rustum," where, while Rustum lay by his dead son, "the majestic river" Oxus floated on

> "Out of the mist and hum of that low land,
> Into the frosty starlight, and there moved,
> Rejoicing, through the hush'd Chorasmian waste,
> Under the solitary moon;—he flow'd
> Right for the polar star, past Orgunjé,
> Brimming and bright and large; then sands begin."

but at last:

> "His luminous home of waters opens, bright
> And tranquil, from whose floor the new-bath'd stars
> Emerge, and shine upon the Aral Sea."

These lines have more poetry than could be distilled from all the rest of "Sohrab and Rustum," but it is not the office of a reconciler to obliterate the parties he is reconciling; in this instance, the father of Sohrab and the order of things which has imposed on him the killing of his own son. So faintly is Rustum, and his tragedy, realized that we forget all about him in this picture of the majestic river floating on. The reconciliation is, characteristically of Arnold, not a reconciliation at all, but an escape.

This fault occurs also, much more flagrantly, in the

elaborate simile at the close of "The Scholar Gipsy,"
the most famous of Arnold's poems. The poem is based
on a seventeenth century story of a young man who,
being forced by his poverty to leave Oxford, joined a
band of gipsies. Arnold imagines him still alive, wandering through the country round Oxford, immune
from "the lapse of hours," because he had retired early
from life "with powers fresh, undiverted to the world
without."

> "O born in days when wits were fresh and clear,
>   And life ran gaily as the sparkling Thames;
>   Before this strange disease of modern life,
>   With its sick hurry, its divided aims,
>   Its heads o'ertax'd, its palsied hearts, was rife.
>   Fly hence, our contact fear!
>   Still fly, plunge deeper in the bowering wood!
>   Averse as Dido did with gesture stern,
>   From her false friend's approach in Hades turn,
>   Wave us away, and keep thy soltitude!
>   Still nursing the unconquerable hope,
>   Still clutching the inviolable shade . . ."

This appeal to the scholar-gipsy to fly "our feverish
contact" closes with the famous simile of the grave
Tyrian trader who, descrying among the Ægean isles
the emerging prow of a merry Grecian coaster, turned
from the intruder on his ancient home, "and day and
night held on indignantly" till he reached the shores
beyond the western straits, and the country of the dark
Iberians.

The inappositeness of the comparison between the

scholar-gipsy and the grave Tyrian trader, and between the o'ertax'd palsied modern and the merry Grecian coaster, exposes once again the weak hold upon Arnold's imagination of any theme not directly related to his experience. Like Rebekah and Moses, the scholar-gipsy is the sentimental fancy of a man oppressed by his environment. So faintly does Arnold apprehend his theme, that immediately after praising the scholar-gipsy for fleeing his world so early, Arnold paints the world he fled from as one where wits were fresh and clear, and life ran gaily as the sparkling Thames (the scholar-gipsy, incidentally, was a contemporary of "Thorough" Strafford, Oliver Cromwell, and Praise-God-Barebones).

But now, though with, I hope, a firmer grip on reality, let me imitate Arnold and close this survey of his chief poetic output on a reconciling note; beginning with these exquisite lines from the poem whose subject-matter I have just criticized in so churlish a fashion:

"But when the fields are still,
And the tired men and dogs all gone to rest,
And only the white sheep are sometimes seen
Cross and recross the strips of moon-blanch'd green,
Come, shepherd, and again begin the quest!"

In his prose, Arnold is fond of the words "puissant" and "grandiose." In his poetry, the word "tired" often occurs with beautiful effect, notably in the line just given, and perhaps even more happily in one of the

few lyrics where his verse sings instead of speaking,
"Requiescat":

> "Her heart was tired, tired,
>   And now they let her be."

The idea of repose, whether in death, or in some
state removed from the moral compulsions and im-
moral enticements of the world, releases the only
spring of inspiration in Arnold which always runs clear.

"So rest, for ever rest, O princely Pair!
In you high church, mid the still mountain-air
Where horn and hound, and vassals never come . . ."

and:

> "Mild o'er her grave, ye mountains, shine.
>   Gently by his, ye waters, glide.
>   To that in you which is divine
>   They were allied."

and:

> "Let me see
> Once more before my dying eyes,
> Bathed in the sacred dews of morn,
> The wide aerial landscape spread,
> The world which was ere I was born,
> The world which lasts when I am dead."

and:

> "Far, far from here
> The Adriatic breaks in a warm bay,

Among the green Illyrian hills; and there
The sunshine in the happy glens is fair,
   And by the sea, and in the brakes.
The grass is cool, the sea-side air
Buoyant and fresh, the mountain-flowers
More virginal and sweet than ours.
And there, they say, two bright and aged snakes,
Who once were Cadmus and Harmonia,
Bask in the glens, or on the warm sea-shore,
In breathless quiet, after all their ills."

XXIV. A HALF-WAY HALT
INCLUDING
A REVIEW OF REVIEWERS

A S I am now half way through this study, a halt for
retrospect on my part and for recuperation on
the part of my readers will do us both good.

It has often been pointed out with surprise that those
most given to dissecting others object most keenly to
any dissection of themselves. Why this should occasion surprise, I don't understand. How many persons
who eat beef with relish enjoy being bitten by cows?
Hardly one in a hundred.

I admit, therefore, without embarrassment, that I
should welcome a sympathetic treatment of this study
by the critics. To facilitate this, I shall set forth as
many objections to my treatment of Arnold as I can
think of, with my reasons for thinking the objections
unsound, acute and admirably expressed though they
are.

Objection No. 1. Mr. A. writes: "A typical product
of our clever young post-war generation, Mr.
Kingsmill, in a section which he entitles, "Sanctity
of Private Life under Queen Victoria," makes
very smart game of such inconsiderable writers as
the late Lord Tennyson, Dickens, Thackeray, and

Thomas Hood. No doubt their attitude towards life was singularly circumscribed. Their minds had not, it must be admitted, been broadened by jazz and wireless, or by the perusal of the works of Mr. James Joyce and Monsieur Victor Marguerite. None the less, we take leave to doubt if the authors of 'Vanity Fair' and 'David Copperfield,' of 'In Memoriam' and 'The Song of the Shirt,' have quite as much reason to hide their diminished heads as Mr. Kingsmill is pleased to suppose.

"But, seriously, is it not about time our younger writers realized that this making game of the Victorians is really rather *vieux jeu?*"

Reply. I am much obliged to Mr. A. for giving me this chance of pointing out that Tennyson and the rest were dealt with, in this section, only in their relation to the Victorian social system, where they appear at their very worst.

Mr. A., like all champions of the Victorian age, assumes that I have criticized it as humdrum and commonplace. On the contrary, I have tried to show how abnormal it was; no more abnormal age in history, indeed, for no other age has had to cope with so rapid and extraordinary an increase in wealth and population as was inflicted on the Victorians by the sudden wholesale introduction of machinery.

The Victorian writers can be properly appreciated only if they are regarded as grotesques of genius. In the section Mr. A. refers to, I had to deal with their grotesqueness apart from their genius. Had it been relevant, I would with equal pleasure have illustrated the genius without the grotesqueness, as in the best of Thackeray and Tennyson, or the genius in grotesqueness, as in Browning and Dickens.

As to Mr. James Joyce, although I admire him greatly, his attitude towards the Victorians has never seemed to me sufficiently detached to be safely adopted. As an instance of what I mean, I refer my readers to the vignette of Queen Victoria in "Ulysses," a book which they may find it difficult to procure in London, the home of Shakespeare, but which they will find on sale in Geneva, the home of Calvin.

The point of view at which I have tried to place myself in my examination of the Victorians is that of the normal civilized European, such as were, apart from their genius, Shakespeare and Cervantes.

When Don Quixote, at the beginning of his adventures, rode up to an inn one evening, two young women, "ladies of pleasure as they are called," were standing outside. They were alarmed by Don Quixote's lance and buckler, and were about to run indoors, when Don Quixote addressed them. "Fly not, ladies, nor fear any discourtesy;

for the order of knighthood, which I profess, permits me not to offer injury to anyone, much less to virgins of such high rank as your presence denotes."

"The wenches, when they heard themselves styled virgins, a thing so out of the way of their profession, could not contain their laughter, and that in so violent a manner, that Don Quixote began to grow angry. . . ."

What would the author of this passage have made of Dickens' unfortunates, vanishing into the night with wild, unearthly cries? Or, to take a less extravagant instance, yet one sufficiently grotesque, what would the creator of Troilus, Pandarus and Cressida have thought of the scene where Rawdon Crawley, a powerful young guardsman, having knocked out a decrepit old lecher, his wife Becky regards him with dazed admiration, "strong, brave, and victorious"?

Objection No. 2. Mr. B. writes: "Mr. Kingsmill's portrait of Dr. Arnold is simply a re-hash of the least successful of the four studies contained in Mr. Lytton Strachey's "Eminent Victorians." Whether Mr. Lytton Strachey's picture of Dr. Arnold was worth the painting is an arguable question. Possibly it was. But we can see no justification at all for Mr. Kingsmill's copy. We would remind Mr. Kingsmill of the apologue of "The Magician's Apprentice."

Reply. I feared this criticism would be made. Like
Mr. B. I regarded Mr. Strachey's portrait of Dr.
Arnold as somewhat of a caricature, and I wel-
comed the chance of showing my superior insight
and sympathy. But the evidence supplied in Dean
Stanley's life of the essential justice of Mr.
Strachey's portrait was too strong for me.

It is a pity Mr. Strachey never varies the look
of blank distaste with which he regards Dr.
Arnold. The humanity in Dr. Arnold, hard to get
at anywhere else, comes out in his desire to rest in
Grasmere churchyard, "under the yews which
Wordsworth planted, and to have the Rotha, with
its deep and silent pools, passing by."

Mr. Strachey misses this, but very little else.
His study of Dr. Arnold is, though short, extraor-
dinarily complete, and had my sketch been merely
a condensation of Mr. Strachey's study it would
have presented Dr. Arnold quite fairly. It was,
however, written before I re-read Mr. Strachey,
whose "Eminent Victorians" I had not looked at
for some years.

Objection No. 3. Mr. C. writes: "Among other
matters of grave concern to Mr. Kingsmill is the
fact that Matthew Arnold not only never lost his
head over a waitress, that was perhaps too much to
hope for, but did not even offer marriage to the
young French lady with the dubious past about
whom Mr. Kingsmill offers us so much interest-

ing, if not particularly well-supported, information. We would suggest to Mr. Kingsmill that, in spite of these omissions, Matthew Arnold made quite a creditable thing of his life. In the three relations of son, husband and father he was altogether admirable, the job of work on which he and his family depended for their support he did as thoroughly as the dullest of us, and a little more brilliantly; and, in his spare time, he managed to give us the best literary criticism of his age, and some of its best poetry.

"That is a record which a good many of us would be proud to claim. To Mr. Kingsmill it is a very painful record. From what heights of virtue and achievement Mr. Kingsmill gazes despondently down on Matthew Arnold we do not know, not having the good fortune to be acquainted with him personally or to know his work, other than this book. And, frankly, this book, in itself, would not appear to justify Mr. Kingsmill's attitude towards one of the major figures of Victorian literature."

Reply. This criticism, the personal element in which I ignore, is very much to the point, but not to the right point.

The fallacy in its argument is that it implies a man is to be judged a success or a failure by comparing his achievement with that of other men, Mr. C.'s, for example, instead of with the possibilities implicit in his own achievement. If the gap between his achievement and what he might have achieved is too wide, he must be judged to have failed.

By this test Goethe, Milton, Matthew Arnold, and H. G. Wells are failures; Shakespeare, Burns, Heine, and Arnold Bennett successes; although Goethe's achievement, for example, is greater than Heine's, and H. G. Wells', on the whole, greater than Arnold Bennett's.

Objection No. 4. Mr. D. writes: "Frankly I can't make out what all the fuss is about. Mr. Kingsmill whips up our excitement by an elaborate defiance to the Victorian convention of biographical reticence, and then, when the least we are entitled to expect is a picture of a little establishment on Lake Como, with a mysterious and bewhiskered Victorian gentleman crooning over the offspring of a secret passion for an Italian Countess, all we get is a vague kiss or two tentatively offered to a French governess, and apparently withdrawn before acceptance. Mr. Kingsmill's right job is compiling primers of literature for the use of the lower forms in girls' schools. He would put the higher forms to sleep."

Reply. I expected this. There is always one critic who, while the rest are making frontal attacks, steals upon one's rear.

Fortunately I am prepared. My objection to the Victorian convention of biographical reticence is not that it always or even usually covers any extraordinary excesses, but that it obscures our understanding of the relation between the Victorian writers and their books. Whether this reticence is employed to cloak an Italian Countess and a love-child, or a French governess and a cold in the head caught through sitting by the lake after sunset, does not bear on my criticism of it.

XXV. MARRIAGE AND FIRST YEARS AS A
SCHOOL INSPECTOR, 1851–1857

ARNOLD'S descent from poet to prophet was accomplished in easy stages, over a long period, from 1851 to 1867. His election to the Professorship of Poetry at Oxford, in May, 1857, may be taken to mark the end of the first stage.

It was his appointment by Lord Lansdowne to an inspectorship of schools that enabled him to marry, in June, 1851. His wife was Frances (Fanny) Lucy Wightman, daughter of Sir William Wightman, one of the judges of the Court of Queen's Bench. Frances Lucy was abbreviated by Arnold to "Flu" in his letters, probably to distinguish her from his sister Fanny.

In a selection from Arnold's Poems, published in 1924, the editor, Mr. Houghton, stated, on the authority of Lady Sandhurst, Matthew Arnold's daughter, that the poem entitled "Calais Sands" refers to Mrs. Matthew Arnold. This poem was published in 1867, but it deals, on any theory of it, with the period before Arnold's marriage, and was probably written round about 1850.

As, until I read this note of Mr. Houghton's, I had always taken "Calais Sands" to refer to Marguerite, and had, therefore, been forced to invent a theory to account for Marguerite's presence so far from Lake

Thun, and had grown in time rather fond of my
theory, I wrote to Mr. Houghton to lay my doubts
before him; and he was so kind as to send me the following answer:

"I have written to Lady Sandhurst, passing on your
query. She insists that "Calais Sands" *was* written to
her mother, and adds that her father was too badly off
to think of marriage till he got his inspectorship. . . .
She says that he followed them about unknown to them!
She again reminds me that Arnold always insisted
'Marguerite' was imaginary. . . ."

To take the last sentence first. Arnold was quite
justified in giving an official explanation to anyone who
bothered him about the Marguerite poems. No author
is obliged to add footnotes to the data about himself
supplied in his writings. His explanation, it now appears, was, like most official explanations, simple and
direct, but, unless understood in a peculiar sense, likely
to mislead. Had he yielded to further inquiries, it
would have been made clear that the poems were imaginary in the sense that Marguerite was not the girl's
real name, that the daughter of the house was not called
Olivia, that Martin was really Walrond, or Wyndham
Slade, and, possibly, that Arnold had first met the
original of Marguerite, not at Thun, as implied in the
poems, but in Paris or on the Lake of Geneva.

The important part of this letter is in the informa-
tion about "Calais Sands." In the final edition of
Arnold's Poems, published by Macmillan, "Calais
Sands" immediately precedes a short series of poems,

under the general title of "Faded Leaves." "Faded Leaves," like "Calais Sands," I had always assumed to refer to Marguerite, though I could not find a completely adequate explanation of the "iron knot" in the following lines:

> " 'Tis true, indeed, an iron knot
> Ties straitly up from mine thy lot,
> And were it snapt—thou lovs't me not!"

In the light of Mr. Houghton's letter, I re-read the "Faded Leaves" series in connection with "Calais Sands," and it is clear that Arnold placed them together for the reason that they both deal with the same girl.

It is very satisfactory to have the "Faded Leaves" series isolated from the "Switzerland" poems, with its simple self-contained story, but some explanation of why I related the two, however tentatively, is perhaps required. I was misled in the first place by that fatal letter on the Clarendon Ministry, the only pre-marriage letter from Arnold to his future wife given us by George Russell. It was a cunning stroke of Russell's, for who would connect the future Mrs. Arnold, plying Matt with questions about Sugden and the Chancellorship, with a series of love-poems? Professor Saintsbury, too, in his study of Arnold, had joined up "Faded Leaves" with "Switzerland." " 'The River' (the first poem of the series) does not name anyone," Professor Saintsbury writes, "though the 'arch eyes' identify Marguerite."

On a closer examination, it is clear that archness is the only connecting link between Marguerite and the girl in "Faded Leaves." Marguerite's eyes are blue, her hair is "soft, ash-colour'd." The girl in "Calais Sands" and in "Faded Leaves" has brown hair, and eyes in one poem grey, in another:

> "Too expressive to be blue,
> Too lovely to be grey."

With a poet so literal as Arnold these differences are decisive, and not only establish that "Faded Leaves" and "Switzerland" do not refer to the same girl, but also identify the girl in "Faded Leaves" with the girl in "Calais Sands."

What possible reason was there for hiding the story of Arnold's engagement? If George Russell and his accomplices had destroyed all Arnold's letters and every fragment of information about him on which they could lay hands, their action would have extorted the praise due to consistency. As it is, two stout volumes of letters witness to their desire that the public should be acquainted not only with Arnold, the writer, but also with Arnold, the man. Or rather, the gentleman, according to a theory of gentility which forbids all mention of poverty as a bar to marriage, and which for Arnold following his future wife, unknown to her, from Calais down the Rhine, substitutes Arnold writing to her as follows: "People speculate on a Clarendon Ministry. If Lord Clarendon comes in, Sugden will

be Chancellor—not else; he is far too much committed on the Papal Aggression question to come in
with a Whig or Peelite Ministry. . . ."

Another, and perhaps my best excuse for failing to
connect "Calais Sands" with Miss Wightman was my
ignorance that Arnold's future was at any time so uncertain as to preclude a formal engagement; and even
had I known this I might not have taken sufficient
account of mid-Victorian conventions to realize that
Arnold, until his prospects were assured, would be
debarred from even addressing the girl he loved. Yet
this was how matters stood at the period referred to in
"Calais Sands," when Arnold was compelled to keep at
a distance, "mixt with the idlers on the pier," during
the disembarkation of Miss Wightman and her father,
Sir William.

> "Thou comest! Yes! the vessel's cloud
>   Hangs dark upon the rolling sea.
>   Oh, that yon sea-bird's wings were mine,
>   To win one instant's glimpse of thee!
>
> "I must not spring to grasp thy hand,
>   To win thy smile, to seek thine eye;
>   But I may stand far off, and gaze,
>   And watch thee pass unconscious by.
>
> "And spell thy looks, and guess thy thoughts,
>   Mixt with the idlers on the pier—
>   Ah, might I always rest unseen,
>   So I might have thee always near?

"To-morrow hurry through the fields
Of Flanders, to the storied Rhine!
To-night those soft-fringed eyes shall close,
Beneath one roof, my queen! with mine."

I am afraid no explanation will altogether excuse the confounding of the heroine of this poem, to whom the deference due an unmarried girl of his own class is so fully paid by Arnold, with Marguerite.

"A sea flows between us—
Our different past."

The lines I have quoted from "Faded Leaves" are now explained.

" 'Tis true, indeed, an iron knot
Ties straitly up from mine thy lot,
And were it snapt—thou lovs't me not!"

The "iron knot" is Arnold's poverty, and the "thou lovs't me not" represents an attempt by Miss Wightman to end an apparently hopeless situation by saying she did not love Arnold; an inference justified, I think, by a later couplet:

"Thy heart is mine! *True, true, ah, true!*
Then, love, thy hand! *Ah no! Adieu!*"

in which her love is confessed, though the impossibility of marriage forces her to dismiss her lover.

The appointment to an inspectorship of schools unloosed the iron knot in 1851, in the June of which year Arnold and Miss Wightman were married. The fairy godmothers of life solve the difficulties of their charges rather more clumsily than the fairy godmothers of fiction. The deep depression of the letter which Matt wrote to his sister "K" about the time of this appointment shows with what little exultation he looked forward to his inspectorship, even though it enabled him to marry. It seems, to quote the first sentence again, "as if we could only acquire any solidity of shape and power of acting by narrowing and narrowing our sphere, and diminishing the number of affections and interests which continually distract us while young, and hold us unfixed and without energy to mark our place in the world; which we thus succeed in marking only by making it a very confined and joyless one."

Joyless Matt's place in the world for the next few years may be called, but not confined. The districts his inspectorship covered included Lincoln, Nottingham, Derby, Stafford, Shrewsbury, Hereford, Worcester, Warwick, Leicester, Rutland, Northants, Gloucester, Monmouth, the whole of South Wales, most of North Wales, and some schools in the East and West Ridings; and the schools he visited were all Nonconformist, and chiefly Wesleyan.

Although Matt would have denied it with as much resentment as his urbanity permitted, there was a good deal of the Dissenter in Dr. Arnold. The unintermittent working of the moral sense, Dr. Arnold's chief characteristic, is one of the saddest features of English Nonconformity. For years, therefore, Matt was immersed in an atmosphere which resembled, however grotesquely, the atmosphere his father had created at Rugby. The apostle of Conduct had conduct in its least engaging forms thrust upon his shrinking notice day after day, for many years. That he held fast to conduct through it all, that he did not one day suddenly take ship for the South Sea Isles, is curious, and perhaps, on the whole, creditable. But the emotional confusion into which he was thrown is shown by the alternation in all his later writings of attacks on Puritanism and uncourtly rebuffs to the Goddess Lubricity.

At first Mrs. Arnold used to accompany him. In October, 1851, during a temporary separation, he wrote to her from Manchester:

"We shall certainly have a good deal of moving about; but we both like that well enough, and we can always look forward to retiring to Italy on £200 a year. I intend seriously to see what I can do in such a case in the literary way that might increase our income. But for the next three of four years I think we shall both like it well enough.

"I think I shall get interested in the schools after a little time; their effects on the children are so immense, and their future effects in civilizing the next generation of the lower classes, who, as things are going, will have most of the political power of the country in their hands, may be so important. . . ."

Two and a half months later he wrote to Mrs. Arnold: "I have had a hard day. Thirty pupil teachers to examine in an inconvenient room, and nothing to eat

~ SWEETNESS AND LIGHT ~
(From a Contemporary Cartoon)
He rebuffed the Goddess Lubricity

except a biscuit, which a charitable lady gave me."

His first child, a boy, Thomas, was born in July, 1852, and it seems that after this date Mrs. Arnold never again accompanied her husband. The expense was too great, and there was a growing family to occupy Mrs. Arnold's attention.

Judging from the references in the letters the first three years or so were those during which Arnold felt the strain and irksomeness of his work most keenly.

"All this afternoon," he wrote to his wife in March, 1853, "I have been haunted by a vision of living with you at Berne, on a diplomatic appointment, and how different that would be from this incessant grind in schools; but I could laugh at myself, too, for the way in which I went on drawing out our life in my mind."

This quotation is as touching as any of his poems— the longing to live within sight of the country of his youthful happiness, and the consciousness that the longing had no relation at all to the reality of things.

At another time he writes: "About four o'clock I found myself so exhausted, having eaten nothing since breakfast, that I sent out for a bun, and ate it before the astonished school," and, two days later: "I am too utterly tired out to write. It certainly was nicer when you came with me, though so dreadfully expensive; but it was the only thing that could make this life anything but positive purgatory." The complaints lessen as he becomes hardened to the work, but eighteen months later there is another glimpse of him in his nomad progress over the vast area between Lincoln and

South Wales. "As cold and uncomfortable a life I have had since I left you as one could desire."

Until 1858, when he and Mrs. Arnold took a house in Chester Square, they had no home of their own. "It will be something," Arnold writes, "to unpack one's portmanteau for the first time since I was married, nearly seven years ago."

There had, however, been periods of rest and domesticity, at Sir William's house in Eaton Place, and at Fox How, Dover, Brighton and elsewhere. The "Quantum patimur" strain, too, even with someone so natural and straightforward as Arnold, is always a little exaggerated in a man's letters to his wife. With the "unquiet breast," of which he speaks, there was a certain advantage for Matt in not being continuously fixed to the hearth. Here is a little picture of him at home, in 1855. He is writing to his mother about a visit his sister Mary had just made to him and Mrs. Arnold. "Dear Mary was invaluable to us, and we have missed her terribly these last two evenings. I so liked hearing her and Flu talk in the evening, as they sate at work while I read. Now all is silence, unless when I sometimes read out a sentence or two."

> "Yes! in the sea of life enisled,
>   With echoing straits between us thrown,
>   Dotting the shoreless watery wild,
>   We mortal millions live *alone*." [1]

The loneliness, for Arnold, was never mitigated by

[1] The italics in the quotations I give from Arnold are always his own.

any close friendships with other men, with a partial
exception in Wyndham Slade, a barrister, to whom
Arnold wrote frequently up till 1856, and with whom
he had travelled on the Continent before his marriage.
His style to Wyndham Slade is much easier than to
anyone else; the anxious moral strain is absent. In 1852
he writes: "I intend coming to the metropolis in a
month's time, and then I hope we shall meet. . . . I
have published some poems, which, out of friendship,
I forbear to send you; you shall, however, if you are
weak enough to desire it, have them when we meet";
and further on he refers to his son, Thomas, then three
and a half months old, as "the child of my declining
years, without brother and sister, unique of his kind."

Two years later he writes from Brussels, which he
describes as "a white, sparkling, cheerful, wicked little
place, which, however, one finds rather good for one's
spirits." There is pathos in that "however."

In 1856 he writes: "The more I see of other trout
streams the more I am convinced of the ineffable
superiority of those in the chalk."

His letters to Wyndham Slade contain many invita-
tions, to Fox How, Dover, and other places; but
Wyndham Slade was never able to accept any of them,
and so the friendship died away through no fault on
either side, though the quotations given show that it was
not rooted in any deep mutual interest.

In 1865, after an interval of many years, Matt wrote
to Wyndham Slade from the Continent. "I shall try
hard to get another look at Salzburg and some part of

the scene of our delightful journey together, which seems only yesterday, and was so long ago."

The letter ends "Ever sincerely yours." In 1852 he signed "Ever yours from the heart," and in 1854 he concludes a letter with: "Write to me, you good soul, and believe me ever yours . . ."

This diminution in the warmth of a youthful friendship is part of the general order of things; but here again there is a lack of tenacity on Arnold's part, as in all his personal relations, outside his relations with his family, which were supported by the social system. Where external support was wanting, Arnold's feeling towards a fuller life was not strong enough to strike permanent roots.

Even with his family, his mother and sisters, and later on his children, most affectionate though his relations with them were, they seem to me never completely intimate, another penalty imposed on him by his epoch, to which, burdened by countless taboos, unconstrained intimacy in the family circle was impossible. In his last years, especially, his love for those children who had survived, is expressed at times with pathetic intensity, but even this relation could not liberate him from his sense of loneliness. It is clear, however, from dozens of passages in his letters that of the happiness he derived from his fellow-creatures on his way through life, the greatest portion came to him from his own children.

Of his four sons, Tom, Budge (Trevenen William), Dick and Basil, Dick alone survived his father. Tom, who was always very delicate, died at sixteen, and Budge at eighteen, and Basil while still a baby.

The first reference of any length to Tom and Budge occurs in a letter from Arnold to "K" in 1857, when Tom was nearly five, and Budge three and a half. "I said to Budge as I was dressing for dinner, 'Budge, you must go and see your Aunt Forster' ("K"). "No," says Budge, "do let me 'top with papa." So I turn to Tom, and when I remind him of the Noah's Ark, Tom says he will go and stop with you 'for two days.' Upon which Budge begins to howl, and running up to Tom, who is sitting on the camp-bed in my dressing-room, entreats him not to go away from him. 'Why not, Budge?' says Tom. 'Because I do love you so, Tiddy Tom,' says Budge. 'Oh,' says Tom, waving his hand with a melancholy air, 'this is *false*, Budge—this is all *false!*' "

Earlier in the same letter Arnold speaks of a proposed visit to Switzerland, which he had not seen since before his marriage. "I have a positive thirst to see the Alps again, and two or three things I have in hand which I cannot finish till I have again breathed and smelt Swiss air. I shall be baffled, I daresay, as one continually is in so much, but I remember Goethe. 'Homer and Polygnotus daily teach me more and more that our life is a Hell, through which one must struggle as best one can.' "

In the previous year he had written to "K" that "to make a habitual war on depression and low spirits, which in one's early youth one is apt to indulge and be somewhat interested in, is one of the things one learns as one gets older."

Although engaged, while only in the early thirties, in this habitual war on depression, it did not occur to Arnold to lay any responsibility for this state on his youthful training. On the contrary: "The more I see of the world," he writes to his mother, "the more I feel thankful for the bringing-up we had, so unworldly, so sound, so pure."

Yet in spite of this pure, sound, and unworldly bringing-up, or because of it, it is hard to say which, he prefers Bulwer Lytton to Charlotte Brontë. The criticism, in a letter to "K," should be read in conjunction with the Preface of 1853, in order to place Arnold as a judge of fiction or of drama.

"Why is 'Villette' disagreeable? Because the writer's mind contains nothing but hunger, rebellion, and rage, and therefore that is all she can, in fact, put into her book. . . .

" 'My Novel' I have just finished. I have read it with great pleasure, though Bulwer's nature is by no means a perfect one either . . . but his gush, his better humour, his abundant materials, and his mellowed constructive skill—all these are great things."

XXVI. MEROPE

IN April, 1856, Arnold wrote to "K": "My poems are making their way, I think, though slowly, and perhaps never to make way very far. There must always be some people, however, to whom the literalness and sincerity of them has a charm."

His election to the Professorship of Poetry at Oxford, in the May of the following year, was a substantial proof that he was already attracting notice. But that he had attracted the notice of Oxford by his literalness and sincerity would be altogether too sanguine a supposition. It was, clearly, the theories set forth in the Preface of 1853, and exemplified in "Sohrab and Rustum" and "Balder Dead," which composed in the minds of those responsibile for his election the qualms raised by the not quite reassuring strain of emotionalism in "The Forsaken Merman" and some of his shorter pieces.

The last vestige of these qualms must have been blown away by the publication of "Merope," in 1858. "Merope" is an imitation Greek drama, the story of which contains the sufficiency of action insisted on by Arnold, being based on one murder and concluding with another. The style in which it is written can be shown in three extracts; the first illustrating Arnold's management of the dialogue, the second his management of the chorus, and the third his management of the action.

1. *Dialogue.*

> *Merope*
> And of his unsure agent what demands
>   he?
>
> *Aepytus*
> News of my business, pastime, temper,
>   friends.
>
> *Merope*
> His messages, then, point not to thy
>   murder?
>
> *Aepytus*
> Not yet, though such, no doubt, his
>   final aim.

2. *Chorus.*

> "But the signal example
> Of invariableness of justice
> Our glorious founder
> Heracles gave us,
> Son loved of Zeus, his father—for he sinn'd.
>
> "And the strand of Euboea,
> And the promontory of Cenæum,
> His painful, solemn
> Punishment witness'd,
> Beheld his expiation—for he died."

3. *Action.* Merope has entered the room of Aepytus,
>   whom she does not know to be her
>   son, and is about to kill him with an

axe. Arcas, an old man of Merope's
household, intervenes.

Arcas

Hold, O Queen, hold!
Thou know'st not whom thou strik'st.

Merope

                  I know his crime.

Arcas

Unhappy one! Thou strik'st—

Merope

                  A most just blow.

Arcas

No, by the Gods, thou slay'st—

Merope

                    Stand off!

Arcas

                    Thy Son!

Merope

Ah! (She lets the axe drop, and falls
insensible.)

Indifferent work may be assigned to some deficiency
in intelligence, but really bad work always illustrates
a weakness, usually the chief weakness, in the writer's
character. Balzac's "Physiologie de Mariage" reveals
the strong element of vulgarity and snobbishness in his
nature; Wordsworth's revised version of the penulti-
mate stanza in "Laodameia" shows the petrification of
his nobler instincts into a callous self-defensive smug-
ness; and Shakespeare, in *Henry V.*, in the Ghost in

Hamlet, and in the frequent mannerisms in his last plays, betrays the strain of pomposity or grandiloquence with which in his less happy moments he sought to balance the social discredit attaching to his profession.

"Merope" is worse than merely flat. There is a touch of perversity in its defiance to every known method of securing a reader's sympathy and attention. As we have seen, his work as school inspector and the circumstances of his life generally were causing Arnold a great deal of discomfort. The instinct, a universal one, to pass his suffering on to others overcame him. His epoch ignored or despised the past, that past of noble and significant actions in which, had it been his fortune to live then, his life would have been so different, so fruitful, puissant, and abounding. Very well! He was Professor of Poetry at Oxford now. Altogether to escape what he wrote was, for quite a large number of persons, impossible. A little drama, then, on the Greek model? Yes, that should meet the requirements of the situation very satisfactorily.

Such, in the background of his consciousness, were his fell ruminations, of which in his normal everyday mood he knew nothing. In July, 1857, he wrote to "K," to whom assuredly he wished no harm: "I must read 'Merope' to you. I think and hope it will have what Buddha called 'the character of Fixity, that true sign of the Law.'" Some months later, in a less sanguine mood, he trusts, in a letter to Madame du Quaire, that his "real love for this form and this old Greek world" has saved him from being "entirely *ennuyeux,* professorial, and pedantic"; and finally, in September, 1858, more than a year after his first letter to "K," he wrote her a second, which is in effect an apology for "Merope": "People do not understand what a temptation there is, if you cannot bear anything not *very good*, to transfer your operations to a region where form is everything. Perfection of a certain kind may there be attained, or at least approached, without knocking yourself to pieces, but to attain or approach perfection in the region of thought and feeling, and to unite this with perfection of form, demands not merely an effort and a labour, but an actual tearing of oneself to pieces, which one does not readily consent to . . . unless one can devote one's whole life to poetry."

It is not, however, as an apology for "Merope" but as a direct contradiction of the 1853 Preface that the passage is chiefly interesting. The classical setting, with its noble and significant actions, appears now merely as the pastime of a man with too little leisure for serious work; while "the region of thought and feeling," which, in reference to Goethe's "Faust," he had, in the 1853 Preface, expressly condemned as a soil of great poetry, he now names as the region where, had the conditions of his life allowed it, he would have tried for perfection in his art.

THE visit to Switzerland, of which he had written so longingly to "K" in the previous year, was managed towards the close of August, 1858. It was eight or nine years since he had seen Switzerland. From Vevey he writes to his wife: "Finally it cleared up as we approached Geneva; at eleven the moon came out, and we saw the tall white houses, with their lights, scattered about the valley of the Rhône, and the high line of the Jura in the distance, beautifully soft and clear. . . . I sat for a little while by my open window, and then went to bed.

" . . . Next morning we were up at seven—a beautiful morning, and there was the exquisite lake before us, with the Rhône issuing out of it, and the sun on the rocky summits of the Jura—all that one thinks of so often when one cannot see them with one's eyes. . . . Mont Blanc in all his glory, with a few clouds playing about the middle of him, but his head and all his long line of Aiguilles cutting the blue sky sharp and bright, without a speck of mist."

The exultation fades out before the close of the letter, which ends: "It seems absurd to tell you, now I have come without you, how I long for you, but so it is. . . . I feel willing to go back at any moment."

However, his spirits rise again; and three days later he furnishes another example of his gift of natural description, a gift without intensity, but always sincere and charming: "The Château de Blonay, an old castellated house standing among those exquisite hills of park and lawn which are interposed between the high mountains and Vevey, and which make Vevey so soft and beautiful."

I have laboured so often Matt's imperfect contact with reality, and inadequate adjustment to life, that I cannot, in fairness, omit the following passage from the same letter:

"I slept for an hour or two, when I woke feeling myself attacked; I had taken the precaution to get some matches from the waiter, not liking the aspect of the bedrooms. I found my enemy and despatched him, but kept the candle lighted."

It was in the course of this journey that Matt stood on the Terrace at Berne, and mused on Marguerite's fate. I have already dealt with his speculation as to whether Marguerite, with her sweet blue eyes, and soft, ash-coloured hair, and smile telling of the unconquered joy of her spirit, had become a prostitute; and I refer to it again merely to point out that for so gratuitous a speculation some excuse may be found in the tone of his epoch, if Arnold was thinking of a real person. But what excuse could cover the grotesqueness of such a speculation if it referred to a mere figure of fancy, imagined in the warmth of his poetic youth?

At the close of his journey, it occurred to him, with a

feeling of relief, that this escape from domesticity to the scenes of his youth had after all afforded only a hollow satisfaction; nor was natural scenery itself really a source of permanent edification. These two discoveries he at once, with the naturalness that was his most endearing quality, communicated to "K."

"I have found two things; one that I am not sure but I have begun to feel with papa about the time lost of mere mountain and lake hunting (though everyone should see the Alps once to know what they are), and to desire to bestow my travelling solely on eventful countries and cities; the other that I miss Flu as a travelling companion more than I could have believed possible, and will certainly never travel again for *mere pleasure* without her."

I N the following spring he was on his travels again,
and again alone, but not for mere pleasure; having
gone appointed Foreign Assistant Commissioner of the
Commission to France and the French-speaking countries—Belgium, Switzerland, etc.—to report on the systems of elementary education there.

"I cannot tell you how much I like the errand," he
writes to "K" in January, in a letter which shows Budge
in a realistic mood. Budge was now six and a quarter.

"She (the governess) said to Budge this morning:
'Who do you love best of anybody in the world?' 'Nobody at all,' says Budge. 'Yes,' says Mrs. Querini, 'you
love your papa and mama.' 'Well,' says Budge."

In February Matt wrote to his sister again, about his
proposed mission, ending, in a momentary forgetfulness
of papa's views on travel: "When I think of the borders
of the Lake of Geneva in May, and the narcissuses, and
the lilies, I can hardly sit still."

His brother, William Delafield, died at Gibraltar in
April, on his way home from India. He was much in
Arnold's thoughts on his journey round France in the
following month, for Arnold commemorates him in two
poems composed or meditated during this time, the one,
"A Southern Night," at Cette, a French port on the
Mediterranean, west of Marseilles, the other, "Stanzas

for Carnac," in South Brittany. "A Southern Night"
opens:

> "The sandy spits, the shore-lock'd lakes,
>   Melt into open, moonlit sea;
> The soft Mediterranean breaks
>   At my feet, free.
>
> "Dotting the fields of corn and vine,
>   Like ghosts the huge gnarl'd olives stand,
> Behind that lovely mountain-line!
>   While, by the strand,
>
> "Cette, with its glistening houses white,
>   Curves with the curving beach away
> To where the lighthouse beacons bright
>   Far in the bay."

Later in this poem Arnold speaks of "the soft Mediterranean side" and "this gracious midland sea."

I quote these two phrases, and the three opening
stanzas of "A Southern Night," to illustrate Arnold's
prevailing tendency in natural description. He draws
from a scene only its tender and composing elements;
and though he is right to keep within the limits imposed by his temperament, the result shows his narrowness of range. This narrowness of range first impressed
me vividly in connection with the lines I have just
quoted:

> "Cette, with its glistening houses white,
>   Curves with the curving beach away"—

lines that had stuck in my mind over many years, until
chance led me for a night to Cette, a squalid port with

the usual noisy mongrel population of "the soft Mediterranean side." As for the Mediterranean itself, "this gracious midland sea," Arnold in praising it is partly seduced by the sound of the word and partly is following a fashion which came in with the Romantic movement at the beginning of the nineteenth century. It is the business of a sea to have tides, not to lounge about like an overgrown lake. Swinburne was the first to point out this truth, in a phrase, "the tideless, dolorous, inland sea," to which one can object only that it is too musical to be wasted on its subject.

From Cette Arnold went up to Brittany, and in the "Stanzas from Carnac" celebrated his unconscious relief at getting away from the Mediterranean. "He tarries" he writes of his dead brother:

> "He tarries where the Rock of Spain
>   Mediterranean waters lave;
> He enters not the Atlantic main.
>
> "Oh, could he once have reach'd this air
>   Freshen'd by plunging tides, by showers!
> Have felt this breath he lov'd, of fair
>   Cool northern fields, and grass, and flowers."

It must be admitted, however, that though inspired by the Atlantic and not by the Mediterranean, this poem is not comparable with "A Southern Night," which closes so exquisitely in a verse I have already quoted:

> "Mild o'er her grave, ye mountains, shine.
>   Gently by his, ye waters, glide.
> To that in you which is divine
>   They were allied."

The "Stanzas from Carnac" are hardly more than a versification of two passages from his letters home. In the first, to his wife, he speaks of the view on the spur of Carnac, by the sea "over the stones and the strange country of the Morbihan (the little sea), and beyond, the bay and peninsula of Quiberon, where the emigrants landed, and beyond that the Atlantic. All this at between six and seven on a perfectly still, cloudless evening in May, with the sea like glass, and the solitude all round entire." And in a letter to his mother, "I thought of Willy the other day at Carnac while I looked over the perfectly still and bright Atlantic by Quiberon Bay, and saw the sails passing in the distance where he would have passed had he lived to come home."

> "Beneath me, bright and wide,
>   Lay the lone coast of Brittany.
>
> "Bright in the sunset, weird and still,
>   It lay beside the Atlantic wave,
> As though the wizard Merlin's will
>   Yet charm'd it from its forest-grave."

The interest of this poem for me is, to recur to a topic which I have perhaps insufficiently laboured, the connection, which Matt of course did not realize, between the subject-matter of the third and fourth stanzas and his own experience at the hands of Dr. Arnold.

> "Behind me on their grassy sweep,
>   Bearded with lichen, scrawl'd and grey,
> The giant stones of Carnac sleep,
>   In the mild evening of the May.

"No priestly stern procession now
    Moves through their rows of pillars old;
No victims bleed, no Druids bow—
    Sheep make the daised aisles their fold."

This acceptance on Arnold's part of the bleeding victims and the bowing Druids as a picturesque primeval happening, in no way related to the universal experience of humanity, or else his meek though, no doubt, unconscious identification of the Druids of Carnac with Dr. Arnold, the Druid of Rugby, or more probably a mixture of the two, constrains me to illustrate my divergence from Matt on the subject of Druids, ancient or modern, by quoting some notes I wrote after a visit to the Menhirs of Carnac in June, 1927.

After some general remarks on sacrifice, the notes continue: "The most important by-product of sacrifice would be the power it gave the priests. It would be to their interest to organize this fear of the gods to the increase of their own importance; and, of course, they would themselves believe in their gods, but rather as magnified projections of themselves than as objects of fear.

"When I was at the Kermario Menhirs, my thoughts went to the victim. The view of the sea and surrounding country is very beautiful from the sacrificial stone. The victim would be chosen, in a primitive society, for his pre-eminence in beauty and strength, primarily on the ground that the best alone was suitable for the gods, but also to gratify the herd's envy of all superiority, or singularity; and especially to satisfy the double envy of the priests, as old men and as the representatives of the herd; for the priest is always with the herd and against the individual.

"The struggle between the individual and society is perfectly symbolized by this old rite of sacrifice. I hope some of the victims refused to submit. There must have been an occasional one who, seeing the distant bay, and remembering some hour of love on its shores, heaved a rock at the infernal high priest and got away into the woods and found his love again.

"On returning to Carnac I saw the funeral of a baby, four girls carrying the tiny coffin. A priest and his acolytes were in attendance to accompany to the grave this little creature who had escaped so quickly from the prison we build with our own hands for our own bondage."

IN 1861 Matt wrote to his mother: "The interest of
the world and of the spectacle of its events as they
unroll themselves is what I regret for him (Dr. Arnold); indeed, this is the main part of what is valuable
in life for anybody."

The chief value of life, that is, consists in everyone
looking at what everyone else is doing. Clearly Matt,
even in 1861, was very nearly in the right mood to set
up as general adviser to the world. I have, however,
taken 1867 as the date of his definite entry into that
office, for that year marked the end of his second term
as Professor of Poetry, and in that year he published his
last volume of poems. Besides, between 1861 and 1867
he was still occupied with literature, publishing within
that period his first volume of "Essays in Criticism,"
and two volumes of Oxford lectures, on "Translating
Homer," and "The Study of Celtic Literature."

Before coming to his literary criticism and his "New
Poems," I shall illustrate from his letters what he made
of the spectacle of events as they unrolled themselves
before him, interspersing here and there glimpses of
his own personal life, an item in the general spectacle
no less significant than any other.

His tour in the spring and summer of 1859 took
Matt through Belgium, of which he wrote to Miss

Arnold: "I dislike Belgium and think the Belgians, on the whole, the most contemptible people in Europe."

Against this verdict I must quote a phrase which has stuck in my mind ever since I came upon it in one of the weeklies, in August, 1914, shortly after the outbreak of the recent war. The author of the phrase, Father Vincent McNabb, was addressing the Kaiser in an open letter, and having told the ensanguined ogre what he thought of him in strong resonant tones, his voice suddenly broke as he turned to the ogre's victim, Belgium —"the little white ewe lamb of Europe."

Matt gives no reasons to explain why in the matter of Belgium he is to be ranged with the Kaiser and against Father Vincent.

It was his desire, he had told "K," to bestow his travelling on eventful countries and cities. A more eventful country, for its size, than Flanders is not to be found in Europe, or more eventful cities than Antwerp, Bruges and Ghent. Nor has Flanders any mountains and lakes to waste a person's time.

From Belgium Matt went to Paris, whence he wrote to his sister that in the event of a war between France and Prussia, France would beat the Prussians all to pieces, even more completely and rapidly than they were at that moment beating the Austrians. Of this, he concludes, "there cannot be a moment's doubt; and they know it themselves;" they being presumably the French, not the Prussians, whose ignorance of France's military superiority lasted throughout the war here forecast by Matt. To his wife he writes that after all he has heard from Sainte-Beuve of George Sand's present proceedings, he does not care to go and see her, a decision of which Mrs. Arnold no doubt approved.

The publicist virus was beginning to work in him. He had recently issued a pamphlet on the Italian situation, of which he wrote to Miss Arnold: "I have often thought, since I published this on the Italian question, about dear papa's pamphlets. Whatever talent I have in this direction I certainly inherit from him, for his pamphleteering talent was one of his very strongest and most pronounced literary sides, if he had been in the way of developing it. It is the one literary side on which I find myself in close contact with him, and that is a great pleasure."

In Paris, beside Sainte-Beuve and Mérimée, he met Ernest Renan, of whom he wrote to "K": "Between his line of endeavour and my own I imagine there is considerable resemblance. The difference is, perhaps, that he tends to inculcate *morality*, in a high sense of the word, upon the French as what they most want, while I tend to inculcate *intelligence*, also in a high sense of the word, upon the English nation as what they most want."

Such was the difference, at this time, between Matt and Renan's lines of endeavour. Later, when Renan tended to inculcate immorality, in a low sense of the word, the difference became much more marked.

On his return to England, Matt joined the Queen's Westminster Rifle Volunteers, and wrote to Miss Arnold that he liked the drilling very much. "It braces one's muscles, and does one a world of good. This Volunteer movement," he goes on to say, "does not arm the people, as some apprehensively imagine. On the contrary, it throws the power into the hands of the upper and middle classes, thus giving these classes the superiority not only of wealth and intelligence, but also of force. I hope and think," he adds, "that the higher classes in this country have now so developed their consciences that this will do them no harm."

The letter continues with some comments on "the English toadyism with which lords and great people are invested with the commands in the corps they join, quite without respect of any considerations of their efficiency"; and concludes with a lament over the "immense vulgar-mindedness, and, so far, real inferiority of the English middle classes."

Poor little Tom, meanwhile, was in perpetual ill-health. In a letter to "K" Arnold says Tom is always coughing and feverish, and whistles because not strong enough to sing.

Budge, while his father was on the Continent, had been "very good at his lessons, being very anxious to have a letter from me, which was to be the reward of his continued industry."

In March, 1861, Matt writes to his mother: "The new baby, or gorilla, as I call her (now Lady Sandhurst), is a fiend at night. She nearly wore poor Miss Young out, and I look forward to the sea to make her a little less restless."

Shortly before the American Civil War broke out, Matt, in a letter to "K," believed that the Southern States meant to go, and would do better by going; and at the close of 1861, at a time when war between England and the Northerners was threatening, he wrote to his mother: "Everyone I see is very warlike. I myself think that it has become indispensable to give the Americans a *moral lesson*, and fervently hope that it will be given them; but I am still inclined to think they will take their lesson without war." Ten days earlier, he hopes that the Americans will not cease to be afflicted "until they learn thoroughly that man shall not live by *Bunkum* alone."

Matt is not to be blamed for being unaware, in 1861, that the newly elected President of the United States did not require lessons in morality from Palmerston or any other mid-Victorian. None the less, the tone of these quotations show how imperfect was Matt's detachment from the popular mood, as soon as that mood became excited; as soon, that is, as detachment became at all difficult. In his attitude towards the American Civil War he is hardly to be distinguished from *Punch* itself. Two years ago I came across a collection of old *Punches* from 1860 to 1890, and went through them with some care.

At the beginning of the Civil War, no one in England expected it to last long, or regarded it with anything but contempt. Carlyle referred to it as a dirty chimney on fire, and disclaimed interest in the foul chimneys of his neighbours. *Punch* showed two urchins fighting in a gutter, and John Bull looking out of the window of his comfortable town mansion, and threatening if they didn't stop their noise to come out and give them both a good thrashing. This warning being ignored alike by Abraham Lincoln and Jefferson Davis, *Punch* became peevish. In the course of the next few years the South was occasionally treated with a touch of condescending sympathy, but Lincoln ("Abe") was always represented as a kind of shiftless, half cunning, half imbecile tramp.

Within two or three weeks of the end of the war, I think after the fall of Richmond, it suddenly struck the English that there was going to be a decisive victory for the North. Accordingly *Punch* converted the gutter urchins into two distinguished-looking gladiators, one of whom is receiving the death-thrust of the other. Underneath is the inscription "Habet."

The next cartoon represented Columbia weeping by an urn in which were reposing the ashes of Abraham Lincoln; and the same number contained the famous verses in which *Punch* expressed its contrition for having maligned Abraham Lincoln. The substance of this apology is curious, being a contrast between the rude uncultivated virtue of one of the few statesmen who have also been great wits and humourists, and the too worldly and sophisticated brilliance of the *Punch* staff between 1860 and 1865.

Between these years, a thorough search did not yield me a single joke on a higher level than the following one, which I quote from memory but without, I think, impairing its merit.

The picture represents an Englishman in a French carriage. The Englishman is making wild gestures to an agitated Frenchwoman. Underneath is an explanation to the effect that this is not a scoundrel threatening murder to a defenceless woman. It is only Mr. Brown of Surbiton trying to explain to a French lady that he would be grateful if she would permit the window to be opened.

I have referred to the politics and humour of *Punch* in the sixties, because it is important, in order to preserve one's fairness towards him, to bear continually in mind that Matt lived in very strange times.

He was especially warped in his attitude to the Civil War by his unconscious distaste for everything and everyone that reminded him of Dr. Arnold. For Napoleon, Richelieu, Cæsar, for Frederick the Great, and even for Bismarck, in spite of Bismarck's piety, Matt at different times expressed an uncritical enthusiasm. But Oliver Cromwell he disliked, and, in his essay on Falkland, criticized his stupidity in not ranging himself with Spain against France, a step which would have strengthened Cromwell's position enormously, owing to the fanatical Catholic sympathies of the army that supported his despotism. The Puritan North, for the same reason, repelled Matt. In 1865 he wrote to "K" with obvious satisfaction: "The students in the Training Colleges had for their composition this year to write a letter from an English emigrant to the United States describing the state of things there, and there is not *really* one per cent who does not take the strongest possible side for the Confederates."

The victory of the North and the circumstances that attended the death of Lincoln modified his hostility for the moment. "What tremendous news this is about Lincoln!" he wrote to his wife. "If Lincoln had been killed two years ago it would have been an immense loss to the North, but now he has done his work. All the recent matters have raised America in one's estimation, I think, and even this assassination brings into their history something of that dash of the tragic, romantic, imaginative, which it has had so little of. *"Sic semper tyrannis"* is so unlike anything Yankee or English middle class, both for bad and good."

But even Lincoln's well-timed and picturesque assassination could not reconcile Matt to him. Nearly twenty years later, Matt ranked General Grant above Lincoln, and complained that the author of the Second Inaugural "lacked distinction."

His letters during this period contain several references to contemporary writers. "Tennyson, with all his temperament and artistic skill, is deficient in intellectual power." "A sort of pseudo-Shelley called Swinburne." "I had some talk with Ruskin, but I should never like him."

At Dover, in 1862, he saw a good deal of Thackeray. "Thackeray," he writes to his mother, "was very amusing, kissing his hand to Flu, and calling me a monster;"

a demonstration of innocent fun which perhaps explains Matt's remarks, in the following year, on Thackeray's death: "I cannot say that I thoroughly liked him, though we were on friendly terms; and he was not to my mind a great writer."

More congenial than any of the writers of the day were Sir Anthony and Lady de Rothschild, whose house, Aston Clinton, near Tring, Matt frequently visited.

"I had a very pleasant day at Aston Clinton with the Rothschilds last Friday," he writes to his mother in 1861, "and a superb game of croquet with the girls. Their croquet things were very grand, and much heavier than ours—you have infinitely more power with the heavy mallets."

With Lady de Rothschild, especially during the sixties, he corresponded quite frequently. "Imagine," he writes to her, "the pleasure of finding out for myself from each of five hundred boys what his father is; and if, as generally happens, he is a tradesman, of finding out besides whether he is a small or great tradesman, and how many people he employs! Such is inspection at present."

An Interlude.

MATTHEW ARNOLD: Your name, if I may ask it.
SMALL BOY: 'Igginbottom, please sir.
MATTHEW ARNOLD: Quite! Your father's occupation? He is engaged in ——? (Pause). What *is* your father?

HIGGINBOTTOM: Grocer, sir.

MATTHEW ARNOLD: Ah! Grocer. On a large scale?

HIGGINBOTTOM: Wot?

MATTHEW ARNOLD: Your father has extensive premises? Or, perhaps, even more establishments than one? (Pause). Has your father *one* shop or *several?*

HIGGINBOTTOM: On'y got one.

MATTHEW ARNOLD: Only one? (Makes a note and looks up with a quick smile.) Thank you, thank you.

From the Highlands, in 1864, he wrote to Lady de Rothschild of his love for the Celtic races, "with their melancholy and unprogressiveness." Why, he asks, does not Sir Anthony take a lodge in the Highlands for two or three years? "Think of the blessing you and your daughters would be to the Highland cabins round you!"

Lady de Rothschild followed his work with interest. "I had read the Preface (to 'Essays in Criticism')," he writes to her, "to a brother and sister of mine, and they received it in such solemn silence that I began to tremble; then —— is always thrown into a nervous tremor by my writing anything which she thinks likely to draw down attacks on me; so altogether I needed the refreshment of your sympathy."

Why George Russell should have omitted "my wife" in this extract, and drawn attention to the omission by the sinister blank, it is now too late to inquire. There are innumerable reasons why a wife should not be able to view her husband's work, whatever it is, with the disinterested appreciation of a woman friend. It would seem, however, that even Arnold's poetry, innocuous though it was, did not find an enthusiastic hearing at home. "My poems," he writes to his mother in 1861, "I am less and less inclined to show or repeat, although if I lived with 'K' I daresay I should never have got out of the habit of repeating them to her."

Meanwhile, Budge, Arnold informs his mother, "had at my instigation buckled to and got a *Bene* for his Syntax, in which, as it was quite new to him, he had been finding great difficulty. The merit of Budge is, though he is an idle dog, that he can, and will, answer to a call."

A little later Arnold has less favourable news: "I am sorry to say he (Budge) and Tom quarrel not unfrequently."

In the summer of '65, Arnold's family joined him on the Rhine. His letters, as usual, show his discriminating eye where scenery was concerned. "The very climate," he writes of the Black Forest, "which carries vegetation up to the top of the hills, prevents their having the bare Alpine summits which make our English hills, even at 3,000 feet, so striking."

He prefers the Rhine, however, "to the monotonous gloom of Windermere," and speaks of it "stretching like a long lake through the country, and the endless towns and spires on its banks."

It is worth noting that Matt seldom, and only as it were, under compulsion, refers to the Lake District with enthusiasm. Here we have him preferring the Rhine to it, and in the previous year he writes, "Wales is as full of traditions and associations as Cumberland and Westmoreland are devoid of them"; and six weeks later he is saying the same of the Highlands.

In the year of this German holiday, Tom was thirteen, Budge nearly twelve, and Dick, ten. Arnold describes them punting in a letter to his mother: "When they strike on a rock Dick or Budge, according as it is in the department of one or the other, flops into the water like a water-rat and pushes the punt off. Dick takes very much to fishing. . . . Budges cares nothing for fishing, and the punt and the river are his great delights. Dear little Tom is wonderfully well, and sits in the middle of the punt with the title of Captain, more for ornament than use. . . . Budge is in an old pair of waterproof leggings which a gentleman has given him."

Tom is always referred to by his father as "little Tom." "Little Tom is going to a fancy-dress dance as Blondel," and, a fortnight later, "Dear little Tom *will* be a *matador*, and he looks well in the dress, but one cannot help smiling at the idea of him fighting a bull or even a frog."

In October, 1865, he sends his mother a story of his daughter Nelly. "She told Mrs. Tuffin to take care of a little comb I had given her—'I wouldn't lose that comb, *for all my means*, Tuffy, because papa gave it me.' "

In the year of the Rhine holiday, Arnold was on the Continent from April to November, on a second official tour. His first halt was in Paris, whence he wrote to his mother: "I miss Flu and the children dreadfully, as you may suppose." To Mrs. Arnold he wrote: "You are quite right in saying I am not enjoying myself." He was, he added, a good deal beat and had nearly lost his voice.

The chief interest of his letters home during this tour is his attempt to school himself into a correct enthusiasm for Italy, most eventful of countries. From Turin he wrote: "Things already have the grand air of Italy, which is so much to my taste." From Florence he wrote to his mother: "You may imagine how I shall think at Rome of dearest papa," though in Rome itself it was Goethe who seems to have been most present to him, as was natural; Goethe being the first and most powerful disseminator, in the modern world, of factitious enthusiasm over Italy. "How I feel Goethe's greatness in this place! Here in Italy one feels that all time spent out of Italy by tourists in France, Germany, Switzerland, etc., is—human life being so short—time misspent."

And at Naples: "My dearest Mother, that is the view, of all the views of the world, that will stay longest with me."

All useless! Once again his sincerity was too strong for him. At Turin, on his return journey, he wrote to "K": "Nowhere has Scotland so gained upon me as here in Italy; the charm of those innumerable clear rivers is so infinite to me"; and to his mother: "The vegetation of the south, splendid as it is, is all *above* the ground and in the branches and leaves of the trees, and not muffling and cooling the ground itself in the way I so love"; and to his wife, also from Turin: "At the end of the streets one sees that glorious wall of the Alps sparkling with snow and ice."

Earlier, in this letter to his wife, he writes: "Since I have been in Italy I have rather wished you wore ear-rings—the great gold ear-rings of this country, in such a variety of styles, please me so much; however, it is perhaps as well you do not."

XXX. DAWNISM

ALTHOUGH Matt's campaign of mental suggestion, in the hope of settling England on a sounder
social, political, and theological basis, did not formerly
begin until he had ceased to be Professor of Poetry at
Oxford, the prose works published before that date
contain a good deal of preliminary skirmishing. This
is therefore a convenient point, before looking at his
earlier prose, to inquire into the reasons which lead certain men to concern themselves with the betterment
of a nation or of mankind in general.

"It is very animating," Matt wrote to his mother in
1863, "to think one has at last a chance of *getting at*
the English public. Such a public as it is, and such a
work as one wants to do with it."

Matt was forty at this time, nor did he sally forth in
good earnest for another four years. No precise age
can be fixed as the appropriate one for coming to the
rescue of mankind. The Indian summer, when the
resolution to make everyone happy restores to a man the
happiness he has lost in his own life, or gives him the
happiness he has hitherto missed, comes to a man early
or late, according to circumstances. Don Quixote was
nearly fifty before he set out for the first time. That
is perhaps a little late, but his temper at fifty was keener
than Matt's at forty, and his methods more direct;

though the scope of their programmes was equally un-bounded.

"Now, these dispositions being made, he would no longer defer putting his design into execution, being the more strongly excited thereto by the mischief he thought his delay occasioned in the world; such and so many were the grievances he proposed to redress, the wrongs he intended to rectify, the exorbitances to cor-rect, the abuses to reform, and the debts to discharge."

Even more than his courage, and apart from his de-lusions, his sagacity, the distinguishing quality of Don Quixote is his egotism. It is for his own personal satis-faction that he sets forth to deliver mankind from its oppressors. Cervantes labours this point so repeatedly that he would not be at all surprised to learn, if he re-turned to life, that Don Quixote had been universally accepted as the type of the selfless enthusiast; which, indeed, he is, if the word "selfless" is understood in the sense suggested below.

It is perhaps the only flaw in Cervantes' conception that he makes Don Quixote so consciously concerned with the aggrandizement of his own dignity and renown. "To be less and less *personal* in one's desires and work-ings is the great matter," Matt wrote to his mother, in 1866, having announced to her, a little earlier: "I mean, as I told Fan in the autumn, to deliver the middle class out of the hand of their Dissenting ministers."

As soon as a man has discovered this distinction be-tween personal and impersonal "desires and workings," his sense of proportion and his consideration for others

diminish; and the selfish instincts he indulged timor-
ously in his own interests begin to be bold, dispensing
him, now that he is working for humanity at large,
from the small obligations of generosity and help to
which the ordinary man is sensitive, even when he fails
to discharge them.

Two men, at an inn where Don Quixote was staying,
on his way to reinstate the Princess Micomicona in her
kingdom, tried to make off without paying their reckon-
ing. The landlord went after them, and they began to
beat him.

"The hostess and her daughter, seeing nobody so dis-
engaged, and so proper to succour him, as Don Quixote,
the daughter said to him: 'Sir Knight, I beseech you by
the valour God has given you, come and help my
poor father, whom a couple of wicked fellows are beating to a mummy.' To whom Don Quixote answered,
very leisurely and with much phlegm: 'Fair maiden,
your petition cannot be granted at present, because I
am incapacitated from intermeddling in any other adventure, until I have accomplished one I have already
engaged my word for; but what I can do for your
service, is what I will now tell you; run, and bid your
father maintain the fight the best he can, and in no wise
suffer himself to be vanquished, while I go and ask per-
mission of the Princess Micomicona to relieve him in his
distress; which if she grants me, rest assured I will
bring him out of it.' "

Such was the response made by Don Quixote, whom
Lamb calls "the errant Star of Knighthood made more

tender by eclipse," to the cries of the landlord and the appeals of his wife and daughter.

I need not labour how closely Don Quixote here pre-figures Rousseau inaugurating the simple life (with, it must be admitted, some show of logic) by sending his bastards to a foundling institution, or Tolstoi refusing to go near his wife in child-birth owing to her infringe-ment of the celibate rule he was preaching to mankind. The knight's general likeness to Robespierre, Crom-well, Lenin and other saviours of humanity also needs no elaborating.

One must, however, distinguish beneath the excessive egotism induced by becoming "impersonal" the virtue that was the original motive power behind these mis-directed enthusiasts. Wealth and high position were not their aims or Don Quixote's. He desired a larger ex-perience than this world affords, or had at least afforded him. He saw near at hand a more abundant life, and promised it to Sancho, as Jesus, whom I think Cervantes often had in mind while writing his book, promised it to his disciples.

Further, Don Quixote and Sancho Panza, though they never reached the fairyland they were looking for, did actually find a fuller life than if they had stayed at home. For the mass of men, stagnation is the normal condition. The choice between stagnation and madness is offered them only at long intervals. When it is, mad-ness is naturally preferred. The kingdom of heaven is not established on earth by wars, revolutions and cru-sades, but these explosions of the accumulated discontent of mankind ease the oppression of life for a moment, and are thus partially justified.

With the mass of men one must class their natural leaders, such as Don Quixote, Cromwell, Moses, Lenin and the rest, who are distinguished from their followers not by a greater detachment from illusions but by their superior courage, energy and resourcefulness.

When we turn to the philosophers and poets, whose business it is to climb up from time to time out of the storm-tormented valley, and, after looking down upon it with tranquil detachment, to bring back to its inhabitants the wisdom they have found on the heights, we find that the proportion of wisdom to illusion in their reflections is smaller than might have been expected. Even more passionately than the others they desire the storm shall cease, and the valley be as calm as the mountain tops, or the strip of sky beyond; and this desire takes shape in prophecies of a day when calm shall descend on the valley for ever, and in assurances, based on an imperfect understanding of natural phenomena, that the storm can be charmed to rest by the inhabitants themselves.

It is an illusion that the storm will ever accommodate itself to the dwellers in the valley; but before examining some of the forms this illusion has taken, it would be well to show the highest authority for the view that those in the valley should accommodate themselves to the storm, instead of trying to persuade the storm to accommodate itself to them.

In "Prometheus," a dramatic fragment, Goethe

makes one character ask another (I quote from memory):

"*Was denn ist mein?*" (What then is mine?)

The other replies: "*Der Kreis den deine Wirklichkeit erfüllt—nichts mehr, nichts weniger*" (The sphere your actual self fills—no more, no less).

Shakespeare expresses the same truth in "Simply the thing I am shall make me live"; and Jesus, who was divided between the search for reality and the desire to force salvation upon mankind, gave as the fruit of the former preoccupation two rules of life—To love God and one's neighbour as oneself.

These three truths from Goethe, Shakespeare and Jesus are in essence the same—to rest in oneself, cultivating one's particular faculty, and to respect one's neighbour's practice of the same virtue. The commandments of Jesus also define the function of love, which is not to be diluted in a thin stream over humanity, but to exercise itself in the concrete realities of daily existence; and, without entangling oneself in the definition of God, one may see among other things in the injunction to love God a promise of a satisfaction beyond this life of the longing for perfection, though the mixed character of Jesus' teaching allows other interpretations.

Unfortunately, to be simply the thing one is, to remain in one's own sphere, filling it with one's actual self, satisfies a very small minority of mankind; although, apart from those with a special faculty for science, invention or art of some kind, the number of persons tolerably contented with their work, however ordinary, is rather larger than a pessimist, like Schopenhauer, hopeful of universal despair, would care to admit.

But the majority of mankind are, like Don Quixote and Sancho Panza, ill-at-ease in their spheres. To be simply the thing they are is exactly what they would prefer not to be. The Sanchos fancy some other sphere than the one they are occupying, and the Don Quixotes feel an impulsion to tidy and re-arrange the contents of every sphere except their own.

In his later years Tolstoi used to affirm that he could not be happy, until he was assured that every other inhabitant of the earth was also happy. That such an inflamed sensibility was not a symptom of virtue but of maniacal egotism did not occur to Tolstoi. The masses, in spite of the temporary aberrations which involve them in wars and revolutions, realize at bottom that happiness alone creates happiness. Tolstoi, who was always praising the masses, never attained even to the good sense, though poor poetry, of "Pack up your troubles in your old kit bag, and smile, smile, smile."

Matt with his gentle nature and divided impulses was only a half-hearted Tolstoi or Don Quixote. "Everything," he wrote to his mother before sallying forth, "depends upon one's exercising the power of *persuasion, of charm.*" That was not Don Quixote's method, nor is this stuff of which an apostle of love, like Tolstoi, is made. Matt's charm never did more than irritate strangers. It had none of the intimate racking quality of Tolstoi's love.

But Matt or Don Quixote or Tolstoi, an imperfect

adjustment to his surroundings is always at the bottom of a man's concern with the general welfare.

Matt had not enough strength to be simply the thing he was, a poet. He succumbed to the hostile forces which had attacked him continuously from the beginning, and he became a prophet; and like other poets turned prophet put the blame for the transformation on his age.

In the night of what he preferred to consider a noncreative epoch nothing remained for him but to look round for the first signs of dawn, an occupation for which history, and especially the Bible, furnished numerous precedents.

Dawnism, or heralding the dawn of a new world, of the millenium, the establishment of the kingdom of heaven on earth, the New Jerusalem, the dictatorship of the proletariat, the Age of Reason, the resurrection of Judæa or Ireland, France, Germany or Russia, etc., etc., in short, an excited anticipation that some form of collective action is about to solve all the troubles of the individual, is an intermittent but apparently incurable malady of mankind.

The essence of dawnism being to escape from the sphere of the individual into an ideal collective sphere, dawnism is most intense where the conditions of life are least favourable to the individual.

In 1921 and 1922, emerging each morning from Euston Square Underground on to the north side of Euston Road, I used to see across the way a large poster, displaying a crowing cock. The poster was an advertisement of *The Daily Herald*, and the cock signified *The Daily Herald's* conviction that the dawn about to rise in Russia under Lenin's supervision would shortly cross over to England. Years passed, and one morn I missed him at the accustomed place. Intellectually I was not in sympathy with him, but I spared him a sigh, as I pictured him rolled up and carted away to be converted to whatever uses waste paper serves.

The years immediately after the Russian Revolution and the close of the Great War, mark one of the great dawnist epochs of history. It was felt that the waste of life and wealth, and the suffering entailed by the war had been so enormous that they could never occur again. Mankind had had its lesson. Its inherent good sense would not permit a repetition, etc.

Although it would be possible to illustrate every phase of dawnism from the speeches of statesmen since 1917, from novelists during that period, and from H. G. Wells, it is perhaps wiser, in conformity with Matt's Preface of 1853, to go for my subject-matter to a distant time and country, with a few supplementary illustrations from the literature of the intervening epochs.

The first recorded instance in history of the dawnist fallacy is the embarkation of Noah, his wife, sons, and daughters-in-law, with a representative selection of animals; the total complement being designed faithfully to reproduce the world that was about to be blotted out as an unsuccessful experiment.

Passing over the failure to construct a tower of escape from earth to heaven, over Lot's disheartening experiences in Sodom, and the various migrations of Abraham and his descendants, we come to the exodus from Egypt to the land flowing with milk and honey, the conquest of which earthly paradise was accompanied by the extermination or enslaving of all the original inhabitants, except Rahab the harlot.

In the centuries that followed this settlement internal dissensions and constant trouble with their neighbours made it hard for the Jews ever to forget the collective in the individual. They lived preoccupied with the necessity of safeguarding their national integrity, and of propitiating their Deity, whose reality for them mirrors their craving to be supernaturally protected against their enemies, and whose brooding presence gives their literature its peculiar intensity while depriving it of humour and imaginative freedom.

In 737 B. C. the Jews entered into the long period of foreign captivities in Assyria and Babylon; and from this time on their literature, the writings of the major and minor prophets, is predominantly dawnist in character.

One of the prophets, Isaiah, was a man of extraordinary genius, who in happier conditions would have created works of sustained greatness. A single phrase shows his genius: "The Lord shall give thee rest from thy sorrow, and from thy fear, and from the hard bondage wherein thou wast made to serve": but this should be a valediction over a representative of universal humanity, such as Lear, a breathing suffering man,

not, as it is, over a political and social unit, personified
only in metaphor.

The world of the Prophets, even of Isaiah, is a madman's dream. The madman cries to a God, glaring from
the sky, now to avenge Israel on Babylon and Assyria,
now to redouble the torture of his own people. The
sun turns into darkness, and the moon into blood. Children are dashed to pieces on the rocks, the beasts groan
and run to and fro, the earth quakes, and the heavens
tremble. A stink rises from the carcasses of the slain,
the mountains are melted with their blood. There is
blood everywhere. The sword of the Lord is filled with
it, made fat with fatness. In the ruined fortresses and
palaces of the earth owls nest and dragons couch, and
across the desolate places the satyr cries to his fellow,
and overhead the vultures wheel.

The horror sinks to mere filth and cruelty. One
prophet, Ezekiel, is steeped in the images of lust;
whoredom, pollution, the discovery of nakedness,
whoredom, nakedness, pollution—the lewd gabble has
no end. Another, Jeremiah, broods over the image of a
tortured baby: "the tongue of the suckling-child cleaves
to the roof of his mouth with thirst." He pictures his
God starving men into cannibals: "And I will cause
them to eat the flesh of their sons, and the flesh of their
daughters, and they shall eat everyone the flesh of
his friend;" or descending from Heaven to play Quilp-
like tricks on His chosen people: "For, behold, I will
send serpents, cockatrices among you, which will not be

charmed, and they shall bite you, saith the Lord."

Presently, beyond this inferno, in images to which horror still clings, a God arises before whom mankind flees "into the clefts of the rocks, into the tops of the ragged rocks, for fear of Him, for the glory of His majesty, when He ariseth to shake terribly the earth." The horror dwindles, God's lineaments are purged of their fiendish cruelty. "They shall not hurt nor destroy in all My holy mountain, saith the Lord." The burden of His presence is still felt, but with lessening terror. He recedes further and further, until all terror is gone. "Thine eyes shall see the King in His beauty: they shall behold the land that is very far off," and at last He is hardly even a presence in Isaiah's vision of a transfigured world: "The wilderness and the solitary place shall be glad for them; and the desert shall rejoice and blossom as the rose. And the parched ground shall become a pool, and the thirsty land springs of water; in the habitation of dragons where each lay shall be grass with reeds and rushes. And the ransomed of the Lord shall return, and come to Zion with songs and everlasting joy upon their heads; they shall obtain joy and gladness, and sorrow and sighing shall flee away."

In this marvellous passage God and Israel are alike submerged in a vision of perfection comparable with the immortal sea of Wordsworth. Here for once the poet in Isaiah triumphs over the prophet. The other prophets never see beyond the bringing again of the captivity of Israel, the affliction of Israel's enemies, and the establishment in Jerusalem of an earthly Utopia presided over by the demon, now pacified, of their nightmares. "In that day shall there be upon the bells of the horses, 'Holiness unto the Lord'; and the pots in the Lord's house shall be like the bowls before the altar." That is, though with a quaint charm rare in dawnist literature, a typical expression of the immemorial dawnist illusion that the kingdom of Heaven will some day materialize on earth.

I have quoted at length from the Old Testament, beginning at the story of the Flood, because in no other literature is the relation between an unhealthy social and political condition and the illusion of human perfectibility so fully and clearly shown. But doubtless there is no country which could not furnish some contributions to the dream of the millennium. In Latin literature there is the fourth eclogue of Virgil, with its prophecy of a Golden Age, "Summer of the snakeless meadow, unlaborious earth and oarless sea," the poem which so recommended him to mediæval Christendom. Even the great humanists loosen their grasp of reality at times, Rabelais in the Abbey of Theleme, and Shakespeare in the sonnet supposed to have been written at the accession of James I.: "And peace proclaims olives of endless age."

But Shakespeare was by nature and by conviction an anti-dawnist, and in his last play, *The Tempest*, written when the Puritans were beginning to advance, Old Testament in hand, on the decaying fortress of the Renaissance, he makes fun of the Utopian in Gonzalo, and of the rank and file of millennialists in drunken Stephano:

"Every man shift for all the rest, and let no man take care for himself," and in Caliban, with his song of freedom on changing one master for another:

> "No more dams I'll make for fish;
>   Nor fetch in firing
>   At requiring,
> Nor scrape trenchering, nor wash dish:
>   'Ban, 'Ban, Ca-caliban,
>   Has a new master: get a new man."

Shakespeare shows the converse of the truth that great imaginative literature is produced with difficulty in nations whose disorder is beyond the normal, a truth I offer to the Irish who are always puzzled by the poor results they have achieved in poetry compared with the gross Anglo-Saxon. The poets of England have not had their energy drained away and their sense of reality warped in the service of a collective emotion. What English poet, except Thomas Campbell, has ever bothered about Britannia? But the finest Irish poem of the nineteenth century is inspired by "Dark Rosaleen":

> "Over dews, over sands
>   Will I fly for her weal.
> Her holy, delicate, white hands
>   Shall girdle me with steel."

The current of dawnism released by the French Revolution ran strongly throughout the nineteenth century. Three instances may serve both to round off this sketch of the nature and influence of dawnism, and to frame Arnold in a contemporary setting of fellow-dawnists.

A streak of dawnism runs through Heine's otherwise individual genius, and finds its highest expression in a poem that forecasts the return of Frederick Barbarossa to lift Germany out of its chaos, and to punish

> "Die Mörder, die gemeuchelt einst
> Die teure, wundersame
> Goldlockigte Jungfrau Germania—
> Sonne, du klagende Flamme!"

In "Le Chasseur Noir" Victor Hugo prophetically obliterates the Czar and Austria and the Pope, all kings, priests, judges, spies, abbots, monks and Kaisers, and of course Napoleon the Third, out of which universal ruin France arises in her old splendour:

> "Tout reprend sa force première,
> Tu redeviens la France altière
> Si belle à voir,
> L'ange blanc vêtu de lumière,
> O chasseur noir!

> "Le clair chant du coc perce les nuées
> Ciel! l'aube apparâit."

Finally, Dostoieffsky interweaves with his studies of Russian murderers, prostitutes and lunatics the constant refrain that the salvation of the world will shortly be accomplished by Holy Russia.

XXXI. MATTHEW IN SEARCH OF A DAWN

ARNOLD'S "New Poems," which appeared in 1867, contain two dominant strains, a sense of fatigue and despair, and the attempt to correct this fatigue and despair with the hope of happier times to come, for the world though not for himself.

The first strain is most fully expressed in "Stanzas from the Grande Chartreuse," the second in "Obermann Once More."

In the "Grande Chartreuse," Arnold tells how he rode up through "the stony forest-way" to the famous Hospice:

> "The silent courts, where night and day
>   Into their stone-carved basins cold
> The splashing icy fountains play—
>   The humid corridors behold!
> Where, ghostlike in the deepening night,
> Cowl'd forms brush by in gleaming white.

> "The chapel, where no organ's peal
>   Invests the stern and naked prayer—
> With penitential cries they kneel
>   And wrestle; rising then, with bare
> And white uplifted faces stand,
> Passing the Host from hand to hand."

The monks' faith had ceased to be his, but he mourns its loss, and he is linked with them in the world's contempt.

> "Wandering between two worlds, one dead,
>   The other powerless to be born,
> With nowhere yet to rest my head,
>   Like these, on earth I wait forlorn.
> Their faith, my tears, the world deride—
> I come to shed them at their side."

He cries to the cowl'd forms to take him and fence him round, till he possesses his soul again.

> "Till free my thoughts before me roll,
>   Not chafed by hourly false control!"

But the hope of this renovation fades at once. The age of Byron, bearing through Europe "the pageant of his bleeding heart," and of Shelley's "lovely wail, musical through Italian trees," is past. "The best are silent now," given over to the inaction of despair, while the modern world thunders exulting by:

> "You give the universe your law,
>   You triumph over time and space!
> Your pride of life, your tireless powers,
>   We laud them, but they are not ours."

In "Obermann Once More," composed, Arnold tells us, many years after the first "Obermann," Arnold is again at Glion, above Lake Neman, and under the Dent de Jaman.

> "Ah, Jaman! delicately tall
>   Above his sun-warm'd firs,
> What thoughts to me his rocks recall,
>   What memories he stirs!"

The memory of Obermann revives, and as he muses

night comes on, and "still and sudden" Obermann
stands near him. You who fled from me, Obermann
says, when the earth lay in gloom, have, then, returned,
in this hour when earth is reborn, and hopes and hearts
bloom again. He sees that Arnold does not quite take
his meaning:

> "Ah! Carry back thy ken,
> What, some two thousand years! Survey
> The world it was then!"

He pictures the Roman world, at the time of Christ's
birth, filled in spite of its power and wealth with disgust and secret loathing, ready for the message from
the East.

> "She heard it, the victorious West,
> In crown and sword array'd!
> She felt the void which mined her breast,
> She shiver'd and obeyed.

> "She veiled her eagles, snapp'd her sword,
> And laid her sceptre down;
> Her stately purple she abhorr'd,
> And her imperial crown——

> "Oh, had I lived in that great day,
> How had its glory new
> Fill'd earth and heaven, and caught away
> My ravish'd spirit too!"

For centuries Christ's force was unspent.

> "While we believed, on earth he went,
> And open stood his grave.
> Men call'd from chamber, church, and tent;
> And Christ was by to save.

"Now he is dead! Far hence he lies
      In the lorn Syrian town;
And on his grave, with shining eyes,
      The Syrian stars look down."

The tide of faith had retired, and a dead world waited
for a freshening storm.

"Down came the storm! O'er France it pass'd
      In sheets of scathing fire;
All Europe felt that fiery blast,
      And shook as it rush'd by her."

But

"It was not yet the appointed hour.
      Sad, patient, and resign'd,
I watch'd the crocus fade and flower,
      I felt the sun and wind."

And now he rests in his humble tomb by the Seine, with,
for sole inscription, "Eternity, be thou my refuge!" But
Arnold he enjoins not to despair, as he had despaired.
The sun has risen, breaking the winter of the past.

"The world's great order dawns in sheen,
      After long darkness rude,
Divinelier imagined, clearer seen,
      With happier zeal pursued.

"With hope extinct and brow composed,
      I mark'd the present die;
Its term of life was nearly closed,
      Yet it had more than I.

"But thou, though to the world's new hour
      Thou come with presence marr'd,
Shorn of the joy, the bloom, the power,
      Which best beseem its bard;

"Though more than half thy years be past,
  And spent thy youthful prime;
Though, round thy firmer manhood cast,
  Hang weeds of our sad time;

"Whereof thy youth felt all the spell,
  And traversed all the shade—
Though late, though dimm'd, though weak, yet tell
  Hope to a world new-made!——

"What still of strength is left, employ,
  That end to help men gain.
*One mighty wave of thought and joy
  Lifting mankind again!*"

The vision ends, Arnold awakes as out of sleep, and
stirr'd by some strange impulse looks eastwards towards

"where in haze
The Valais opens fair,

"And the domed Velan with his snows
  Behind the upcrowding hills
Doth all the heavenly opening close
  Which the Rhone's murmur fills—

"And glorious there, without a sound,
  Across the glimmering lake,
High in the Valais depth profound,
  I saw the morning break."

This is a beautiful close; but it is impossible to endorse
the connection suggested by Arnold between the dawn
rising over the Valais, and the new world of which
Matt, "though late, though dimm'd, though weak" is

adjured by Obermann, over-sanguine for once, to be the John the Baptist.

In the first place, the logic of the poem demands that the French Revolution, "the freshening storm" reviving the dead corpse, should inaugurate the new world. Certainly no event or series of events between the French Revolution and the composition of this poem in the middle of Queen Victoria's reign could compete with the French Revolution as a dawnist phenomenon. But the logic of the poem also demands that the event inaugurating the new world should have an overwhelmingly restorative effect. (One mighty wave of thought and joy lifting mankind again!) Such an effect could not be attributed to the French Revolution by the cheerless Obermann.

> "It was not yet the appointed hour.
>   Sad, patient, and resign'd,
> I watch'd the crocus fade and flower,
>   I felt the sun and wind."

But logic or no logic, some kind of a dawn Matt is determined to extract out of the modern world from which he has just taken refuge in the Hospice of the Grande Chartreuse. If he can do nothing else, he can at any rate help mankind to lift the wave that is presently to lift mankind.

It is a relief to turn to the days when his melancholy had as yet no need to the dawnist anodyne.

> "Farewell! Under the sky we part,
>   In this stern Alpine dell!
> O unstrung will! O broken heart!
>   A last, a last farewell."

SOME humble-minded dawnist, if one exists, equally impressed and discouraged by the last few pages, will be murmuring—"But his attitude is purely negative? Is, then, all human effort valueless?"

There is a mean between fluttering after the millennium, and dissolving into Nirvana under a banyan-tree; the mean indicated by Goethe in his maxim that each man should confine himself to his own sphere.

Arnold's sphere was poetry and literary criticism. The exquisite work he did in poetry, as long as he kept within his limits, has been fully illustrated. In literary criticism the temptation to stray beyond his limits was naturally much stronger. There was always the world waiting to be put in order to distract him from the matter in hand; and the distraction was the more tempting because he was far more interested in the world than in its inhabitants, the chief theme of literature.

His "Lectures on Translating Homer" were Arnold's first critical work of any length.

Arnold's abasement before Homer is as profound as before Moses and Rebekah. Homer, he urges, is always rapid, always plain and direct in style, always noble. Anything in Homer that seems inconsistent with these qualities is to be regarded as not being inconsistent with these qualities. "Homer always composes as Shake-

speare composes at his best; Homer is always simple
and intelligible, as Shakespeare is often; Homer is
never antiquated, as Shakespeare is sometimes."

Having settled these points, Arnold continues: "So
essentially characteristic of Homer is his plainness and
naturalness of thought that to the preservation of this
in his own version the translator must without scruple
sacrifice, where it is necessary, verbal fidelity to his
original, rather than run any risk of producing, by
literalness, an odd and unnatural effect. The double
epithets so constantly occurring in Homer must be dealt
with according to this rule; these epithets come quite
naturally in Homer's poetry; in English poetry they, in
some cases if not often, come, when literally rendered,
quite unnaturally. I will not now discuss why this is
so, I assume it is an indisputable fact."

Therefore, when Homer speaks of one-hoofed horses,
the translator must "speak of horses in a way which
surprises us as little as Shakespeare surprises us when
he says, 'Gallop apace, you fiery-footed steeds!' When
Homer says that life is 'as honey pleasant,' the English
reader should be guarded against the shock of this,
to him, fanciful image, by some such phrase as Gray's
'warm precincts of the cheerful day.' When Homer
introduces Priam 'armed with good ashen spear,' the
disturbance to English sensibilities must be avoided by
calling Priam just 'warlike.' "

Having thus enforced upon the translator the necessity of being without scruple, Arnold, who has previously set forth his reasons for preferring the hexameter

to any other English metre for translating Homer, illustrates the combined effect of unscrupulousness and the English hexameter in the following specimen translation:

"So shone forth, in front of Troy, by the bed of Xanthus,
Between that and the ships, the Trojan's numerous fires.
In the plain there were kindled a thousand fires: by each one
There sat fifty men, in the ruddy light of the fire:
By their chariots stood the steeds, and champed the white barley
While their masters sat by the fire, and waited for morning."

"I omit," Arnold says, "the epithet of morning, and whereas Homer says that the steeds 'waited for morning,' I prefer to attribute this expectation of morning to the master and not to the horse. . . . Homer's lively familiarity with war, and with the war-horse as his master's companion, is such that, as it seems to me, his attributing to the one the other's feelings comes to us quite naturally; but, from a poet without his familiarity, the attribution strikes as a little unnatural; and therefore, as everything the least unnatural is un-Homeric, I avoid it."

How a translator of Homer, if, like Arnold, unfamiliar with war, ought to deal with the violence usual in hand-to-hand fights, whether a bitter retort, say, or a veiled innuendo should be substituted for a sharp thrust through the midriff, Arnold does not tell us. Why, indeed, Homer himself, unless he had some theory about noble and significant actions, ever dealt with such barbarous matters is puzzling, for the final impression Matt gives of Homer is that Homer was very like Matt:

"When one observes the boisterous, rollicking way in which his English admirers love to talk of Homer and his poetry, one cannot help feeling that there is no very deep community of nature between them and the object of their enthusiasm. 'It is very well, my good friends,' I always imagine Homer saying to them, if he could hear them, 'you do me a great deal of honour, but somehow or other you praise me too like barbarians!' "

XXXIII. CELTS AND TEUTONS

IN his lectures on Celtic Literature, Arnold had a subject far more closely related to his temperament than Homer. They open by his describing, with a charm which sets the key of the book, the view to the west as he had seen it during a visit to Llandudno. "Over the mouth of the Conway and its sands is the eternal softness and mild light of the west; the low line of the mystic Anglesey, and the precipitous Penmaenmawr, and the great group of Carnedd Llewelyn and Carnedd David and their brethren fading away, hill behind hill, in an aerial haze, make the horizon; between the foot of Penmaenmawr and the bending coast of Anglesey, the sea, a silver stream, disappears one knows not whither."

The fashion of ascribing all our virtues to our German stock had, except in the History School at Oxford, passed away some years before the outbreak of the Great War reminded us that we were, like our cousins the French, of Latin origin. After the unification of Germany by Bismarck, it became increasingly hard to see the Germans as a nation composed exclusively of chaste, corpulent and tearful dreamers, whose only temptations were a glass of beer and a well-filled pipe. But until the 'seventies this conception of Germany ruled in England.

The German victory in the Franco-Prussian war was, Charles Kingsley said, "the triumph of Christianity and the Gentle Life."

To the Englishman as Christianized Teuton, Tennyson, speaking on behalf of his age, opposed the lewd and fickle Gaul ("the red fool-fury of the Seine"; "Art with poisonous honey stolen from France") and the emotional and shiftless Celt ("the schoolboy heat, the blind hysterics of the Celt").

Arnold was hampered, in his attempts to change this view of the French, by their undoubted lubricity. This difficulty did not exist with the Irishman. "The Frenchman," he wrote to Monsieur Fontanès, in 1873, "is a latinised Irishman," and he goes on to say that while the Celt in Ireland is chaste "le Celte latinisé, le Français, est tout autre chose. Selon Sainte-Beuve, Proudhon disait que 'la France était tournée toute entière vers la fornication.'"

Arnold was further drawn to the Celts by his father's dislike and disapproval of them. "Can you show me a single line," he wrote to his mother, in 1866, "testifying to his (Dr. Arnold's) sense of any virtues and graces in the Celt?"

"I remember, when I was young," he says in the first lecture, "I was taught to think of Celt as separated by an impassable gulf from Teuton; my father, in particular, was never weary of contrasting them; he insisted much oftener on the separation between us and them than on the separation between us and any other race in the world."

In his youth, he continues, in a passage of extraordinary interest in view of his later year-long efforts to elevate the Bible above all other literature, "the Jew—the Jew of ancient times, at least [1] seemed a thousand degrees nearer than the Celt to us—a steady, middle-class Anglo-Saxon much more imagined himself Ehud's cousin than Ossian's. But, meanwhile, the pregnant and striking ideas of the ethnologists about the true natural grouping of the human race, the doctrine of a great Indo-European unity, comprising Hindoos, Persians, Greeks, Latins, Celts, Teutons, Slavonians, on the one hand, and, on the other hand, of a Semitic unity and of a Mongolian unity, separated by profound distinguishing marks from the Indo-European group and from one another, was slowly acquiring consistency and popularising itself."

In illustration of the profound separation of the Indo-European from the Semitic group Arnold quotes, with some shrinking, William von Humboldt's antipathy to Semitism, with its "absorbing, tyrannous, terrorist religion." This seems to Arnold an extreme case of Indo-Europeanism, yet, "even in this sphere," he admits "the tendency is in Humboldt's direction."

Having placed the Jew in one great racial group, and the Englishman and the Celt in another, Arnold goes on, in what is, on its political and sociological side, the main theme of the book, to draw the connection between the Englishman and the Celt much closer than anyone had yet ventured to draw it. Arnold was the first, at

---

[1] An important qualification.

any rate in popular literature, to see the absurdity of the view held by Freeman and his school that the Saxons, when they invaded Britain, completely exterminated the Celtic inhabitants. "Surely it must strike with surprise anyone who thinks of it, to find that without any immense inpouring of a whole people, that by mere expeditions of invaders having to come over the sea, and in no greater number than the Saxons, so far as we can make out, actually came, the old occupants of this island, the Celtic Britons, should have been completely annihilated, or even so completely absorbed that it is vain to seek after Celtic elements in the existing English race."

To reinforce this argument, which is now a commonplace, Arnold illustrates the difference which this presumed mixture of Celt and Saxon, later complicated by the Norman infusion, has established between the Englishman and the German. He compares the straightforward prose style of the English and the involutions of German prose. He adduces the German supremacy in volume of intestines ("and who," he asks, "that has ever seen a German at *table d'hôte* will not readily believe this?"); and he contrasts an English moral tale for children, exemplifying the virtues of thrift, prudence and foresight, with a German story of a king's chamberlain who, when complimented by a stranger on his wealth and happiness, asked the stranger to take an apple from its golden vessel and cut it in half.

The guest obeyed, "and behold, in the middle of it there was a worm! Then the stranger looked at the chamberlain; and the chamberlain bent his eyes on the ground and sighed."

"One sees there," Arnold comments, "an abyss of platitude open, and the German nature swimming calmly about in it, which seems in some way or other to have its entry screened off for the English nature. The English story leads with a direct issue into practical life, a narrow and dry practical life, certainly, but yet enough to supply a plain motive for the story; the German story leads simply nowhere except into bathos."

Finally, Arnold shows the different impression made on the French by the Englishman and the German. The German the French qualify as *balourd*, heavy and dull, the Englishman as *empêtré*, hampered and embarrassed; and Arnold quotes a remark of George Sand's: "Nearly every Englishman, however good-looking he may be, has always something singular about him which easily comes to seem comic—a sort of typical awkwardness in his looks or appearance, which hardly ever wears out."

In the dangerous task of generalizing about national characteristics, Arnold here keeps his eye with unusual concentration on concrete instances, and presents them with considerable humour. As a result, this book influenced opinion more than any of his other books, except perhaps the first series of "Essays in Criticism." The change in the attitude of the educated Englishman both towards the Irish and the Germans between 1870 and the Great War owed a great deal to Arnold.

The qualities in the Celt to which Arnold directs the

attention of the mid-Victorian Englishman are his sensibility and delicacy of perception. "They went forth to the war, but they always fell." This quotation from Ossian is the keynote of the Celt, according to Arnold; but, he adds, "do not let us wish that the Celt had had less sensibility, but that he had been more master of it." The Englishman, Arnold argued, was in no danger of imitating the Celt's "reaction against the despotism of the established fact," and could safely and with advantage submit to an infusion of Celtic sensibility and grace.

As the Teuton tradition of the nineteenth century began to break up, this counsel of Arnold's was taken to heart by the cultured English. Between the beginning of the twentieth century and the Great War, it was hard to find any English person of the reading classes whose mother, or father, or at least one grandparent, was not of Irish birth; nor did the change of attitude towards the Irish produced during this period by Bernard Shaw make a strain of Irish blood any less of an asset. Irish blood was equally agreeable to its possessor whether he held the Irish to be a charming, sensitive, over-worldly race, or hard-headed realists with an amused if slightly disgusted contempt for the sentimental Englishman.

The events in Ireland since the Great War, by providing the Irish with a government of their own, have deprived them of their picturesqueness. Since they can no longer be yearned over as ineffectual dreamers, or admired as detached cynics, it is difficult to see by what formula a successor to Arnold and Shaw could stem the present tendency of the cultured Englishman to be dervied from parents of English extraction.

On its sociological side, then, the effect of Arnold's book, though valuable at the time, was ephemeral. Its chief interest is as an expression of Arnold's own nature. The son of the practical and energetic Dr. Arnold was inevitably drawn towards a race who whenever they went forth to the war always fell. In the "eternal softness and mild light" of the Celtic west Matt was glad to hide himself from time to time from the Hebraic obligations of morality, practice, and conduct.

"We are none the better," he says, "for trying to make ourselves Semitic, when Nature has made us Indo-European, and to shift the basis of our poetry."

The basis of this poetry, he argues, is far more Celtic than has been hitherto realized; and the Celtic element in English poetry, in spite of critics who maintain that, at any rate in the Welsh language, there are no traces of a pagan mythology, derives from pre-Christian, primeval origins.

"What are the three hundred ravens of Owen, and the nine sorceresses of Peredur, and the dogs of Annwn, the Welsh Hades, and the birds of Rhiannon, whose song was so sweet that warriors remained spellbound for eighty years together listening to them? What is the wonderful mare of Teirnym, which on the night of every first of May foaled, and no one ever knew what became of the colt? Who is the mystic Arawn, the king of Annwn, who changed semblance for a year with

Pwyll, prince of Dyved, and reigned in his place? These are no mediæval personages; they belong to an older, pagan, mythological world?"

The Celtic imagination seems to Arnold to draw from greater depths than the Teutonic, to be nearer the origin of things, and therefore to have a magic in its interpretation of nature not found in Teutonic poetry or even in Greek.

"Magic is just the word for it—the magic of nature; not merely the beauty of nature—that the Greeks and Latins had; not merely an honest smack of the soil, a faithful realism—that the Germans had; but the intimate life of nature, her weird power and her fairy charm. As the Saxon names of places, with the pleasant wholesome smack of the soil in them—Weathersfield, Thaxted, Shalford, are to the Celtic names of places, with their penetrating, lofty beauty—Velindra, Tyntagel, Caernarvon—so is the homely realism of German and Norse nature to the fairly-like loveliness of Celtic nature."

The German poets, Arnold says, treat of nature with faithful realism. They lack Greek radiance and Celtic magic, both of which qualities are found in English poetry, the Greek note in Keats'

> "What little town by river or sea shore,
>   Or mountain-built with peaceful citadel,
>   Is emptied of its folk, this pious morn?"

and in Shakespeare's "I know a bank where the wild thyme blows. . . ."; the Celtic note in Keats'

"Magic casements, opening on the foam
     Of perilous seas, in faery lands forlorn"

and in Shakespeare's

"In such a night
Stood Dido, with a willow in her hand,
Upon the wild sea-banks, and waved her love
To come again to Carthage."

In this criticism there is a subtlety of perception, deriving from Arnold's poetic nature, blunted every now and again by the same cause which prevented him from understanding Wordsworth's Ode. The passage I have quoted in which he summarizes the Celtic myths is filled with a longing towards the primeval world, which is also the world of a child's imagination. That this world was muffled for Arnold in his early years I have suggested in connection with a passage from a letter to his mother—"I looked affectionately in the bright morning towards Fledborough; my recollections of it are the only approach I have to a memory of a golden age." It seems to me that in his desire to repair this loss he fixed on the Celtic imagination with special eagerness because within its sphere he was removed as far as possible from Dr. Arnold's influence. Hence the defiantly exclusive right to natural magic which he claimed for the Celtic imagination. Natural magic, or, to define it more clearly, the sense of the ecstasy or horror outside normal existence, is not a peculiar gift of any race, but a sense present in some degree, however faint, in everyone throughout life, though most strongly felt in childhood; and reproduced with greatest intensity in poets whose imagination had not matured, in Blake and Coleridge, for example, and in some of the old ballads. Shakespeare's imagination is mature; so, on the whole, is Keats'. There is a faint suggestion of a stage property about the notorious casements; and Dido, with a willow in her hand, is a marvellous Renaissance picture, but there is no strangeness in the picture, none of the "fairy dew of natural magic" ascribed to it by Arnold.

At the same time not only individuals but some peoples, too, have this sense far more intensely than others, and Arnold illustrates this excellently in his contrast between Saxon and Celtic place-names. In the imaginative not in the moral sense of the word, there is an other-worldliness in the Irish, not found to the same degree in any other European people, and drawn out so strongly in them, perhaps, because they lived for so many thousands of years at the extreme edge of the world, on the edge of a shoreless sea.

Arnold's tendency, already noticed with Homer, and still more extravagantly shown in his later dealings with the Bible, to overpraise, from his standpoint, whatever object he is prostrating himself in front of for the time being, is shown in this book, too. To take Byron, the most energetic and successful of all publicity-agents, and Milton's Satan as two examples of the Celt's indomitable reaction against the despotism of fact is curious.

> "What though the field be lost?
> All is not lost; the unconquerable will,

> And study of revenge, immortal hate,
> And courage never to submit or yield,
> And what is else not to be overcome."

"There, surely," says Arnold, "speaks a genius to whose composition the Celtic fibre was not wholly a stranger."

It is true that, owing to the exceptional circumstances of the case, Satan's defeat was certain, even before the enemy was engaged, but the spirit of his defiance is a perfect specimen of Teuton doggedness crossed with Hebrew savagery.

XXXIV. OBJECTS AS IN THEMSELVES THEY
REALLY AREN'T

THE first essay in Arnold's "Essays in Criticism" sets forth Arnold's view of the function of criticism, both in general and in relation to his own age.

Criticism, he says, is "a disinterested endeavour to learn and propagate the best that is known and thought in the world." "It is the business of the critical power in all branches of knowledge, theology, philosophy, history, art, science, to see the object as in itself it really is."

Disinterestedness—that is the quality in himself as critic which Arnold requested the world to recognize. "The critic must keep out of the region of immediate practice in the social, political, humanitarian sphere, if he wants to make a beginning for that more free speculative treatment of things, which may perhaps one day make its benefits felt even in this sphere, but in a natural and thence irresistible manner."

This quality of distinterestedness seemed to Arnold to be lacking in his brother-prophets. Cobbett, for example, was blackened with the smoke of a life-long conflict in the field of political practice. Mr. Carlyle had made a furious raid into this field with his "Latter-Day Pamphlets." Mr. Ruskin's political economy was pugnacious.

Elsewhere in this essay Arnold attacks, among other

things and persons, Sir Charles Adderley and Mr. Roebuck, contemporary English Literature, the British Constitution, Bishop Colenso, and the Liberal party.

If this kind of thing constituted disinterestedness, why, someone might have asked Arnold, did he deny the quality to Cobbett, Carlyle, and Ruskin? To which he would have replied, with a charming smile, that he was disinterested because he saw the object as in itself it really was. Had the inquirer asked on what grounds he claimed to see the object as in itself it really was, he would have replied—because of his disinterestedness. I postulate great patience in the inquirer, who would at last have constrained Arnold to adduce, as proof of his detachment and impersonal outlook, the urbanity, the tact, and the courtesy with which he handled the objects of his criticism; in short his persuasion and charm, as he had called them to his mother.

There is no direct evidence of what Arnold thought about the reactions which his charm and persuasion produced in the objects of them. Yet he must have been perplexed at times; for the letter to his mother proves that his charm and persuasion were not deliberate instruments of torture. What, for example, did he think of the *Saturday Review's* remarks on his Homer lectures? "We cannot help expostulating with Mr. Arnold on the tone of his lectures. . . . The bitterly contemptuous language of Mr. Arnold, verging sometimes on personal abuse, sometimes on low buffoonery, does seem to us utterly out of place. . . . All is spoilt by his outrageous self-conceit. The whole of the Lectures are one constant I—I—I."

No application of self-hypnosis, surely, could convince the object of this remonstrance that his charm and persuasion had quite come off that time.

Yet, in spite of the *Saturday Review*, we find Arnold handling Sir Charles Adderley and Mr. Roebuck exactly as he had handled Francis Newman in his lectures on Homer.

"Sir Charles Adderley says to the Warwickshire farmers: 'Talk of the improvement of the breed! Why, the race we ourselves represent, the men and women, the old Anglo-Saxon breed, are the best breed in the world. . . .'

"Mr. Robuck says to the Sheffield cutlers: 'I look around me and ask what is the state of England? . . . I ask you whether, the world over or in past history, there is anything like it? Nothing. I pray that our unrivalled happiness may last.'

"Now obviously," Arnold comments, "there is a peril for poor human nature in words and thoughts of such exuberant self-satisfaction, until we find ourselves safe in the streets of the Celestial City.

> " ' Das wenige verschwindet leicht dem Blicke,
>   Der vorwärts sieht, wie viel noch übrig bleibt, '

says Goethe; 'the little that is done seems nothing when we look forward and see how much we have yet to do.' Clearly this is a better line of reflection for weak humanity, so long as it remains on this earthly field of labour and trial.

"But neither Sir Charles Adderley nor Mr. Roebuck is by nature inaccessible to considerations of this sort. They only lose sight of them owing to the controversial life we all lead, and the practical form which all speculation takes with us."

Unquestionably men of the Adderley and Roebuck type would have preferred the most violent invective to this delicate handling, as of mental cases—"Yes, you believe yourself to be a two-headed ostrich with a stomach of reinforced concrete. A most interesting, and, from some angles, salutary view, but if you would just step this way, and glance at yourself in this mirror, I think it may occur to you . . ."

It is useless to be charming and persuasive without a basis of personal sympathy, and Arnold's personal sympathies were extremely limited. In this instance, as in numerous others throughout his controversial career, the veneer of charm and persuasion soon wore through, showing the contempt and distaste underneath.

"Let criticism confront with our dithyramb this paragraph on which I stumbled in a newspaper immediately after reading Mr. Roebuck—'A shocking child-murder has just been committed at Nottingham. A girl named Wragg left the workhouse there on Saturday morning with her young illegitimate child. The child was soon afterwards found dead on Mapperly Hills, having been strangled. Wragg is in custody.'

"Nothing but that; but, in juxtaposition with the

absolute eulogies of Sir Charles Adderley and Mr. Roebuck, how eloquent, how suggestive are those few lines!"

Arnold draws out the suggestiveness of this juxtaposition over a page and a half, until the plain minds of Sir Charles and Mr. Roebuck can have held only one thought: which of the two is this infernal blighter getting at over Wragg?

Even outside "the region of immediate practice" (and if the attempt to woo Sir Charles and Mr. Roebuck to higher things with a quotation from Goethe is not immediate practice, what is?), Arnold treads very insecure ground in this exposition of his critical faith.

Having, like Empedocles, "laid the use of music by," he wishes to give an air of necessity to his abandonment of creative for critical work.

"The exercise of the creative power in the production of great works of literature or art . . . is not at all epochs and under all conditions possible; and therefore labour may be vainly spent in attempting it, which might with more fruit be used in preparing for it, in rendering it possible." Here is the same idea as in "Obermann Once More," where Matt set before himself the task of helping mankind to lift a wave to lift mankind. It is true that some epochs are more favourable to poetry than others, but these epochs are not inaugurated by lists of themes suitable for creative treatment drawn up in the previous generation by a body of disinterested critics. Criticism follows creation, and corrects it. The baby cannot be beaten till it is born. This fallacy of Arnold's, that criticism precedes creation, is frequently used nowadays by those who, finding themselves unable to create, do not see how the mystery can be explained on any other ground than the presumed unsuitability of the age to the exercise of the imaginative faculty. Hence the present fashion of towardness—Towards a New Poetry, Towards a New Religion, Towards a New World.

"The elements," Arnold continues, "with which the creative power works are ideas." In 1853 the elements with which the creative power worked were noble and significant actions.

Nothing illustrates the personal bias, the lack of disinterestedness, in Arnold's criticism more forcibly than this complete change of front. He had tried and failed to prick on his creative faculty with noble and significant actions, in "Sohrab and Rustum," "Balder Dead" and "Merope"; and having failed he now decides that the age is hostile to imaginative work, that it is lacking in ideas, that ideas are the root from which imaginative work springs, and that, debarred through no fault of his own from creating masterpieces, he will clarify the age intellectually and so prepare the way for an imaginative Renaissance—"It is the business of the critical power to make an intellectual situation of which the creative power can profitably avail itself."

The barren age from which Arnold purposed to deliver English literature, included, taking the fifty years preceding the appearance of "Essays in Criticism," the best work of Keats, Shelley, Dickens, Carlyle,

Thackeray, Tennyson, Meredith ("Modern Love"), Swinburne and Browning. The fifty years of creative activity inaugurated by Arnold in these essays are represented by Thomas Hardy, the novels of Meredith, the æsthetic movement of Oscar Wilde, the sociological movement of Shaw, Wells and Galsworthy, and imperialism articulate in Kipling. What Arnold's age suffered from was not sterility but congestion, producing in its writers, Dickens, for example, Tennyson and Thackeray the distortion of which examples have been given. Instead of examining the causes of this distortion, from which he himself was suffering, and thereby certainly benefiting himself and perhaps his contemporaries, Arnold, oppressed as usual by his immediate surroundings, decided that "not very much of current English literature, I fear, comes into this best that is known and thought in the world." The "intellectual situation" he desired to create could be created only out of foreign materials.

"There is so much inviting us!—what are we to take? What will nourish us in growth towards perfection?" What, in short, were the objects which seen as in themselves they really are would most quicken the torpid contemporaries of Browning, Balzac and Tolstoi?

The first objects were the French Academy, which already existed, and an English Academy, not yet in being. "Well, then, an institution like the French Academy—an institution owing its existence to a national bent towards the things of the mind, towards culture, towards clearness, correctness, and propriety in thinking and speaking, and, in its turn, promoting this bent—sets standards in a number of directions, and creates, in all these directions, a force of educated opinion, checking and rebuking those who fall below these standards, or who set them at nought."

Throughout this essay on "The Literary Influence of Academies," Arnold is partly seeing in an English Academy that external support he always craved, and partly solacing himself with the idea of a body of Matthew Arnold directing English literature, and checking and rebuking English writers. But somewhere in the depths of his consciousness he realized that there were limits to what England, "the weary Titan," could endure; so at the close of the essay he beats a decorous retreat: "An Academy quite like the French Academy, a sovereign organ of the highest literary opinion, a recognised authority in matters of intellectual tone and taste, we shall hardly have, and perhaps we ought not to wish to have it." As a witness to the advantages of an academy like the French one, he had called Sainte-Beuve; but in the essay on Sainte-Beuve he wrote for "The Encyclopædia Britannica," Arnold, with the inextinguishable honesty that is one of his most attractive qualities, quotes Sainte-Beuve to this effect: "All these academies, between you and me, are pieces of childishness; at any rate the French Academy is. One least quarter of an hour of solitary reverie or of serious talk, yours and mine, in our youth was better employed; but as one gets old one falls back into the power of these nothings; only it is well to know that nothings they are."

The next two essays, occupying a fifth of the book, are concerned with Maurice de Guérin and his sister Eugénie. How is it that, after in his first essay preparing his readers to be shown by the only disinterested critic in England samples of the best that was known and thought in the world, and after in his second essay still further reducing the confidence of his readers in any English critic except himself, Arnold had the audacity to lead forward these two charming though mournful pigmies and present them to an audience on strain for giants of the intellect and the spirit? It was the unconscious audacity of love. As he had ranked Obermann with Goethe and Wordsworth, so he now ranked Maurice de Guérin with Keats, and doubted if Eugénie could "exactly be classed with Pascal." Read not as criticism but as autobiography by proxy, these two studies are most attractive. The de Guérins, unlike Abraham Lincoln, had distinction. They were well-born, cultured, preoccupied with religion, and grateful for the retreat from a coarse and ill-bred world offered by nature. In short, they were very like Arnold, and of better family; so he must be excused for not seeing them as in themselves they really were.

After these essays on the de Guérins, it is unnecessary to bring forward any more proofs that Matt's elaborate parade of distinterestedness was merely an attempt to delude both himself and his readers into the belief that his judgments were an impersonal breathing forth of truth, and in no way an expression of his own likes and dislikes.

All criticism is finally self-expression, and valuable therefore in direct proportion to the critic's feeling and experience; a platitude which Arnold, with his need of external support whether in the form of academies or a sense of disinterestedness, did not see; yet, owing both to his sincerity and to his narrow range, the autobiographical basis of his criticism is especially easy to recognize.

In this volume, for example, there are three studies, of Marcus Aurelius, Joubert and Heine, from which a fairly complete portrait of Arnold could be pieced together.

Marcus Aurelius seems to Arnold "perhaps the most beautiful figure in history." This is a view with which Marcus Aurelius would not have quarrelled even if his principles had permitted him to quarrel. "From my mother," he writes, in a quotation given by Arnold, "I learnt piety and beneficence, and abstinence not only from evil deeds but even from evil thoughts; and further, simplicity in my way of living, far removed from the habits of the rich. . . . From my tutor I learnt endurance of labour, and to want little, and to work with my own hands, and not to meddle with other people's affairs, and not to be ready to listen to slander." And elsewhere, more concisely, "Short is the little which remains to thee of life. Live as on a mountain.

Let men see, let them know, a real man, who lives as he was meant to live."

Arnold finds two flaws in Marcus Aurelius, that he persecuted the Christians, and that he had for a son the brutal and dissolute Commodus. His persecution of the Christians Arnold excuses on the ground that they were represented to Marcus Aurelius as a sect politically subversive and morally abominable. He is not, therefore, to be condemned; yet this mistake seems to Arnold characteristic of Marcus Aurelius. "In his character, beautiful as it is, there is something melancholy, circumscribed, and ineffectual. . . . He is blameless, yet, in a certain sense, unfortunate."

Nor is he to be blamed for Commodus. "Still," Arnold says, "we cannot help wishing that the example of Marcus Aurelius could have availed more with his only son." It seems to have availed too much, if one assumes, as one reasonably may, that Commodus took his father as an example of what to avoid. Yet one can excuse almost any form of debauchery in a son whose father's mode of enjoyment was as follows: "When thou wishest to delight thyself, think of the virtues of those who live with thee; for instance, the activity of one, and the modesty of another, and the liberality of a third, and some other good quality of a fourth."

As an example of liberality Marcus Aurelius could always muse on his wife, who had many lovers; a point not mentioned by Arnold, though he may have had it in mind when he said that Marcus Aurelius was not to be blamed for Commodus.

To show this nut-cutlet Cæsar in his true proportions it is enough to set a single quotation from Johnson's talk by the side of any of the extracts quoted above.

What signifies, someone said to Johnson, giving halfpence to common beggars? They only lay it out in gin or tobacco. "And why," said Johnson, "should they be denied such sweeteners of their existence? It is surely very savage to refuse them every possible avenue to pleasure, reckoned too coarse for our own acceptance. Life is a pill which none of us can bear to swallow without gilding; yet for the poor we delight in stripping it still barer, and are not ashamed to show even visible displeasure, if ever the bitter taste is taken from their mouths."

The good sense in this outburst, to say nothing of the heart in it, kills any stoic maxim you put near it. But Arnold preferred the Stoics, and, though a poet, saw himself in Marcus Aurelius, thus measuring his failure in life. George Russell, in the introduction to the Letters, records how he called on Arnold, when Tom died. "I was with the bereaved father on the morning after the boy's death, and the author with whom he was consoling himself was Marcus Aurelius."

Of this scene, Marcus Aurelius open on the writing table, and George Russell coming in at the door, one can say nothing except: "He is blameless, yet, in a certain sense, unfortunate."

Arnold saw himself also in Joubert, a French critic,

whose "soul had, for its basis of operations, hardly any body at all"; or rather, as with Marcus Aurelius, Arnold saw himself as he aspired to be. With persons constitutionally free from the temptations of the flesh Arnold felt himself, though always with a faint under-current of resistance, happy and at ease, and in a mood to admire with hardly any critical reservations.

Joubert, thinking of himself, speaks of "spirits far less concerned for glory than for perfection, who, because their art is long and life is short, often die without leaving a monument, having had their own inward sense of life and fruitfulness for their best reward."

"There is something a little too ethereal in this," Arnold says, the side of him that did not admire the abnegation of those unable to enjoy momentarily roused. Yet, the protest made, he finds grounds for justifying Joubert: "By not trying to fit his ideas into a house—by being quite single-minded in his pursuit of perfection, perhaps he is enabled to get closer to the truth of the objects of his study, and to be of more service to us by setting before us ideals, than if he had composed a celebrated work."

"With the fever of the senses," Arnold quotes from Joubert, "the delirium of the passions, the weakness of the spirit; with the storms of the passing time and with the great scourges of human life—hunger, thirst, dishonour, diseases, and death—authors may as long as they like go on making books which shall harrow our hearts; but the soul says all the while, 'You hurt me.'"

This Arnold calls "a sentence, worthy of Goethe, to

clear the air at one's entrance into the region of literature." Unfortunately it clears the earth, too; if not of the de Guérins, and Marcus Aurelius, Joubert, and Arnold, yet of Shakespeare, Dante, the author of the Book of Job, Cervantes and Goethe himself.

In 1830, on the outbreak of a French Revolution, Heine, who was at the time on the north coast of Germany, wrote a prose poem, beginning, "I am the Sword. I am the Flame," and continuing with a picture of himself surrounded by the dead bodies of his friends, but victorious. "There is time neither for mourning nor for triumph. The trumpets sound again. The battle breaks out afresh. I am the Sword. I am the Flame."

This is the side of Heine which Arnold pronounces to be the significant side "for us, for the Europe of the present century."

"Taking," Arnold continues, "that terrible modern weapon, the pen, in his hand, he passed the remainder of his life (from 1830) in one fierce battle. What was that battle? the reader will ask. It was a life and death battle with Philistinism."

It was in this essay that Arnold introduced into England from Germany the term "Philistine." This word was his chief contribution to the process of disintegrating Victorianism. It has, in our more self-conscious age, fallen out of use, though I have sometimes heard it employed by one Philistine as a term of contempt for another; but in its day it did good service.

Arnold defines a Philistine as a "strong, dogged, un-enlightened opponent of the chosen people," a definition which, when one reflects what the chosen people were like, raises a doubt about the justice of using Philistine as a synonym for an enemy of art and culture.

"Heine's theatre of ideas," Arnold continues, "was Germany, whose Philistinism does not consist in her want of ideas, or in her inaccessibility to ideas, for she teems with them and loves them, but, as I have said, in her feeble and hesitating application of modern ideas to life. Heine's intense modernism, his absolute freedom, his utter rejection of stock classicism and stock romanticism, his bringing all things under the point of view of the nineteenth century, were understood and laid to heart by Germany, through virtue of her immense, tolerant intellectualism, much as there was in all Heine said to affront and wound Germany."

Here is the dawnist in full throat. How mute him? One hardly knows where to begin in such a complicated enterprise. First of all, there is this picture of a nation teeming with ideas and loving them. That is too big. I cannot handle it. Then there is the picture of this nation, conscious that it is not applying its ideas to life, and looking round for someone to help it in this task. This, too, I pass by. Lastly, there is the picture of Heine, bringing all things under the point of view of the nineteenth century and thereby greatly recommending himself to Germany, in virtue of her immense, tolerant intellectualism.

In the last twenty-five years of his life, Heine visited

Germany only once, and then was careful to keep off Prussian territory, for fear of imprisonment. No poet I have read of has been so exhaustively abused by such of his fellow-countrymen as were aware of his existence; in Heine's case perhaps one in fifteen hundred, for her was widely known. On the political side he was attacked as a traitor in the pay of the French Government. The religious hated him, if Jews, as a renegade; if Christians, as a Jew and a blasphemous sceptic, and Jews and Christians united to execrate his private morals. Such was the attitude of one in fifteen hundred of his fellow-countrymen during his lifetime, and though the bitterness has now died away it has not been replaced by knowledge. In twenty years I have never met a German, however well acquainted with Goethe and Schiller, who knew anything of Heine's later poems.

Supported in this fashion by his own country, Heine's literary creation was, Arnold points out, a success, whereas Byron and Shelley's were failures; and the literary creations of Wordsworth, Keats and Scott, though far more solid and complete than Byron and Shelley's, "have this defect—they do not belong to that which is the main current of the literature of modern epochs, they do not apply modern ideas to life; they constitute, therefore, *minor currents*."

Shakespeare, on the other hand, lived in an age "when English society at large was accessible to ideas, was permeated by them, was vivified by them." He was "powerfully upheld by the intelligent sympathy of the great English middle-class."

I should like to have shown this passage to Shakespeare, as he listened to the drunken sailors bawling down the road from Sackerson's bear-pit, on their way to the rare new piece with half a dozen murders and suicides in it, and an old man's eyes put out on the stage itself, right in front of you.

Or his comments on the intelligent sympathy of the great English middle-class might have been worth the risk of interrupting him as he sat down to the fourth act of *Timon:*

> "Let me look back upon thee. O thou wall,
> That girdlest in those wolves, dive in the earth,
> And fence not Athens! Matrons, turn incontinent,
> Obedience fail in children! Slaves and fools,
> Pluck the grave wrinkled senate from the bench,
> And minister in their steads! To general filths
> Convert, o' the instant, green virginity!
> Do't in your parents' eyes!"

Here and there in this essay Arnold awakes from his dawnist trance, and ceasing for a while to consider in what sense, and with what reservations, Heine was "a brave soldier in the Liberation War of Humanity," treats him as a poet; a man, that is, whose gift intensifies the sense of life in those capable of reading him with sympathy; the only form of liberation a poet can confer, and the highest form of liberation that can be conferred by anyone.

Heine attracted and repelled Arnold in equal degree. His intense life warmed Matt's chilled soul. Matt was fascinated by his wit and humour, qualities faintly discernible in a repressed and distorted form in his own talent; and above all he was drawn to Heine by his pathos—"Heine's sweetest note, his plaintive note, his note of melancholy." But Heine's soul, unlike Joubert's, had for its basis of operations a great deal too much body for Matt. Lubricity, according to Matt, hardens a man's heart; a theory to which he recurred frequently in his later years. So in his poem on Heine, "Heine's Grave," he asks:

> "But was it thou—I think
> Surely it was!—that bard
> Unnamed, who, Goethe said,
> Had every other gift but wanted love?"

It was not Heine. It was Count von Platen whom Goethe criticized as wanting love; a charge, curiously enough, brought against von Platen by Heine also, who, using "want" in a different sense from Goethe, set forth at length and not too delicately what kind of love it was that von Platen wanted.

At the close of his essay Arnold is more detailed and more acrimonious. "He died, and has left a blemished name; with his crying faults—his intemperate susceptibility, his unscrupulousness in passion, his inconceivable attacks on his enemies, his still more inconceivable attacks on his friends, his want of generosity, his sensuality, his incessant mocking—how could it be otherwise? . . . Goethe says that he was deficient in *love;* to me his weakness seems to be not so much a deficiency in love as a deficiency in self-respect, in true dignity of character."

In another essay in this volume Arnold adds the last touch to his composite portrait of Heine, whom he pictures at the close of his life covering himself and the universe with the red fire of his sinister mockery.

Much of what Arnold says both in praise and dispraise of Heine is true; but the total result is completely incoherent, through lack of any central standpoint in the critic himself, who shifts in his examination of Heine from dawnist to poet and from poet to son of Dr. Arnold.

Heine, to summarize this chaos, was wanting in love or at any rate in self-respect, and he was engaged during the last two-thirds of his career in a life and death battle with Philistinism; he was unscrupulous and ungenerous and a master of pathos; and, finally, he was a kind of pantomime Mephistopheles, vanishing through a trap-door with a fiendish laugh.

"Lay on my coffin a sword; for I was a brave soldier in the Liberation War of Humanity." Heine was vain and theatrical. All his defects both in his life and his work can be traced to this central weakness, the obverse of which was an intense sympathy, not strongly enough based to bear, as with Shakespeare, supreme poetic results, but during the long illness ending in his death purged of most of the vanity that obscured it in his earlier years.

Arnold, however, having briefed himself for Puritanism v. Lubricity, preferred to wind up his case with

the red fire of Heine's sinister mockery rather than with
a quotation from Bimini, the exquisite poem in which
Heine, after years of torture, said his unembittered
farewell to life.

I give as close a translation as I can manage of three
of the concluding stanzas, to serve as a footnote to
Arnold's "sinister mockery."

> "While for youth he thus was seeking
> Daily he became much older,
> Till with wasted frame, and wrinkled,
> He attained at last the land—
>
> "The still land where flows a river
> Under shadowy cypress trees,
> And though mournful is the river
> There is healing in its waters.
>
> "Lethe is the river's name.
> Drink thereof, and thou forgettest
> All thy trouble, yea, forgotten
> Is the sum of all thy sorrows."

XXXV. DON MATTHEW
(1867–1877)

A RNOLD ceased to be Professor of Poetry at Oxford in 1867. No longer hampered by an official position, and having through his official position acquired a certain reputation and authority, he considered the moment ripe for his adventure. So forth he sallied, mounted on Zeit-Geist, a hobby horse, his right hand gently twirling Charm, a lance without a point, and on his head, reminder that he was, after all, a don of Oxford, not of La Mancha, the mortar-board of Persuasion.

It would be tedious to follow in detail his wanderings during the next ten years; nor shall I pause to record the names of those who disliked the shape of his headgear, and reacted in the contrary sense when tickled by his lance, and found the winning but fixed smile of Zeit-Geist rather wearing to the nerves. The relation of the Crusade to the character of the crusader is all that concerns us here.

He opened the Crusade with "Culture and Anarchy," which was published in 1869.

Its whole scope, he says, "is to recommend culture as the great help out of our present difficulties; culture being a pursuit of our total perfection by means of getting to know, on all matters which most concern us, the best which has been thought and said in the world."

Total perfection was neglected by the Englishman, his tendency being to Hebraize, which Arnold defines as "the effort to win peace by self-conquest." This tendency, indispensable as it was, ought to be supplemented by Hellenizing, "the effort to see things as they really are." These two tendencies, working together in harmony, produce the perfect man, and Culture "is not satisfied till we *all* come to the perfect man; it knows that the sweetness and light of the few must be imperfect until the raw and unkindled masses of humanity are touched with sweetness and light."

Of the obstacles to the production of the perfect man, the Nonconformists were one of the most serious. In them the tendency to Hebraize, that is, "to sacrifice all other sides of our being to the religious side," was unbridled. The members of a national church, Arnold urges, are not exclusively concerned with their religious side. "To be a member of a national Church is in itself a lesson in religious moderation, and a help towards culture and harmonious perfection." But with the Nonconformist, "the precious discoveries of himself and his friends for expressing the inexpressible and defining the indefinable in peculiar forms of their own cannot but, as he has voluntarily chosen them, and is personally responsible for them, fill his whole mind."

The member of an Establishment is in contact with the main current of national life, the Nonconformist is not. Hence "the undeniable provincialism of the English Puritans and Nonconformists."

Not only was the Nonconformist provincial and lacking in that command over his religious zeal which distinguishes the ordinary church-goer. Also he did not understand Jesus, as Arnold explained in a later book, "Saint Paul and Protestantism," the argument of which is that Saint Paul's view of Jesus while exactly the same as Arnold's, and, broadly, the same as the Church of England's, was entirely different from the Nonconformist view. Puritanism held that Jesus died to appease an angry God's wrath against mankind; St. Paul, Arnold, and, on the whole, the Church of England, that Jesus died to the law of selfish impulse, for our sake, not his.

A general union of Christendom was, Arnold said, the thing to aim at; for the time being, however, he would be content with a union of Protestants. "But this union will never be on the basis of the actual Scriptural Protestantism of our Puritans." The first step towards this union was for the Nonconformists to understand the Gospel; after which they would join the Church of England and shed some of their provincialism.

Another obstacle to the production of the perfect man was the class-sense. In one section of "Culture and Anarchy" Arnold arranges the English in three categories, the Barbarians (the aristocracy), the Philistines (the middle classes), and the Populace. How remove some at any rate of the barriers between these three categories? "In each class there are born a certain number of natures with a curiosity about their best self, with a bent for seeing things as they are. . . . In general, by the extrication of their best self as the self to develop, and by the simplicity of the ends fixed by them as paramount, they hinder the unchecked predominance of that class life which is the affirmation of our ordinary self."

By checking the predominance of class life men of this stamp open the way for State action, the action of the collective nation, in which Arnold sees the solution, on the practical side, of our difficulties; provided the individuals composing the nation have followed the course of culture already outlined. "Well, then, what if we tried to rise above the idea of class to the idea of the whole community, *the State*, and to find our centre of light and authority there? . . . We want an authority, and we find nothing but jealous classes, checks, and a deadlock; culture suggests the idea of the *State*. We find no basis for a firm State-power in our ordinary selves; culture suggests one to us in our *best self.*"

I have taken 1877 as the date at which Arnold's crusade ended, because in that year he published his "Last Essays on Church and Religion," his final word on that subject, and returned to literature in an essay entitled "A French Critic on Milton." With politics, even after 1877, he still occupied himself occasionally, bringing out in 1882 a volume, "Irish Essays," in which he attributed the English difficulties in Ireland to our lack of charm, and our lack of charm to the fact that our middle-class school were not a public service with the organization and guarantees of a public service. Once or twice, too, he attempted to purge Liberalism of its faults, not seeing that a Liberalism purged of its faults would have to be wheeled about in a bath-chair, and could therefore not help him with his dawn. Much as he disliked the Liberals he had some hopes of them, and none of the Tories. "The Tories," he said, "have not the secret of life and of the future for us."

The secret of the future, as we have seen, was a firm State-power with its basis in our best selves. With this formula Matt began his political campaign and with another formula, clothing the same thought, he may be said to have closed it: "We must *dis*materialise our upper class, *dis*vulgarise our middle class, *dis*brutalise our lower class."

This process he really believed Prussia was carrying through in Germany. The Prussian victory over Austria in the Seven Weeks' War of 1866, followed by the defeat of France in 1870, diverted much of Arnold's admiration to Prussia from France. France's fall, he wrote to his mother in 1871, "is mainly due to that want of a serious conception of righteousness and the need of it, the consequences of which so often show themselves in the world's history." In a satirical work, "A friendship's Garland," a series of letters first published in the *Pall Mall Gazette* and later issued in a volume, Arnold gave through the mouth of Arminius Von Thunder-ten-Tronckh, a descendant of the Baron in "Candide," his idea of how England would strike a Prussian whose impressions of England were identical with Arnold's. The moral of the book is in this sentence of Arminius': "I have told you our German programme—*the eleva-*

tion of a whole people through culture. That need not be your English programme, but surely you may have some better programme than this your present one—*the beatification of a whole people through clap-trap.*"

In his polemical writings Arnold always comes forward as a plain man, with no skill in abstract reasoning, but with a kind of instinct for reality, formed by a certain amount of reading in the best authors. This attitude soon wearies in his serious writing, but in "Friendship's Garland" he manages the contrast between himself in the character of a mild, blundering, Grub Street hack and his dogmatic Prussian mentor with enough skill to indicate reserves of humour of which, had he developed along other lines, he might have made good use.

There is humour, and, in a sketchy unfinished way, a touch of macabre fancy in his account of the burial of Arminius, shot on outpost duty near Paris. Arminius is discovered by a young Lion of the *Daily Telegraph*, who persuades three English members of Parliament, breakfasting in the summer-house of a villa near by, to help him to dispose of Arminius' remains. They do not like the job, but at last consent, after first stipulating that what they were about to do should on no account be drawn into a precedent.

"It was a hurried business, for my friends had an engagement to lunch at Versailles at noon. Poor Von Thunder-ten-Tronckh, the earth lies light on him, indeed! I could see, as I left him, the blue of his pilot-coat and the whity-brown of his hair through the mould we had scattered over him."

Arnold was in the middle forties when he wrote "Culture and Anarchy." He was nearly fifty when he published "Literature and Dogma," and in the intervening period his views on the relative proportions of Hellenism and Hebraism in the perfect man had been strongly modified in favour of the Hebraistic element.

Arnold had argued, in his "Lectures on Celtic Literature," that we were none the better for trying to make ourselves Semitic, when Nature had made us Indo-European. Religious sentiment was the basis of Semitic poetry, the imaginative reason was the basis of Indo-European poetry; and for us to try to shift the basis of our poetry was to oppose ourselves to the irresistible force of a natural law.

This book on Celtic Literature was, as I have shown, a very unfilial affair altogether; and that sentence "we are none the better for trying to make ourselves Semitic" is mere mutiny. Matt's remorse appears first in "Culture and Anarchy," plea though it is for Hellenism. "We English, a nation of Indo-European stock, seem to belong naturally to the movement of Hellenism." But there was "an essential unity in man," illustrated by that "likeness in the strength and prominence of the moral fibre, which, notwithstanding immense elements of difference, knits in some especial sort the genius and history of us English, and our American descendants across the Atlantic, to the genius and history of the Hebrew people."

It is the knitting by this strong and prominent moral fibre of the English and the Hebrews, and the paramount importance of keeping them so knit, which form the theme of "Literature and Dogma," and its companion volume, "God and the Bible." In some respects the Spirit of the Age (Zeit-Geist) seemed to be working for the unknitting of this bond. The masses, to the distress of the Church of England, were "lapsing." They were beginning to listen to Professor Huxley, and Professor Huxley had recently said that if these islands had no religion at all, it would not enter into his mind to introduce the religious idea by the agency of the Bible. But Zeit-Geist was not really with Professor Huxley. Zeit-Geist shared the distress of the clergy over the lapsed masses. But the masses would never be reclaimed as long as the clergy insisted on miracles. "Miracles do not happen." Here Zeit-Geist stuck fast. Bland and gentle, but absolutely unbudgeable. *"Miracles do not happen."*

Miracles being thus disallowed, and the Bible, the bond by which the English and the Hebrews were knit together, being to that extent discredited, the unique character of the Bible had to be placed on another basis, a basis which Zeit-Geist would not disallow.

This basis was Conduct. "Of conduct, which is more than three-fourths of human life, the Bible, whatever people may thus think and say, is the great inspirer; so that from the great inspirer of human life the masses of our society seem now to be cutting themselves off. . . . No people ever felt so strongly as the people of the Old Testament, the Hebrew people, that conduct is three-fourths of our life and its largest concern. . . .

Religion deals in conduct; in three-fourths, therefore, at the very lowest computation, of human life. The only doubt is whether we ought not to make the range of conduct wider still, to say it is four-fifths of human life, or five-sixths. . . ."

This doubt Matt usually controlled, and rested content with three fourths of life for conduct, assigning the other fourth not to misconduct, but to art, science, and philosophy. The proportions of Hellenism and Hebraism in the perfect man were therefore now fixed at one fourth and three fourths respectively.

Why had the Bible suddenly taken on this extreme importance as a guide to conduct? In "Culture and Anarchy," Arnold quotes Mr. T. Chambers, who, speaking on behalf of his bill for enabling a man to marry his deceased wife's sister, asked: "Does God's law forbid us to marry our wife's sister?" This bill of Mr. Chambers' is a theme to which, for some years, Arnold recurs again and again, always with extreme distaste. The measure, it seems, had strong Nonconformist support; and Arnold would shrink from the picture of a well-to-do Dissenting tradesman on his second nuptial night, joining in prayer with his ex sister-in-law before availing himself of the renewed mercies vouchsafed him by the Almighty.

God's law, as set forth in the Book of Leviticus, opposing no obstacles to the marriage of a Nonconformist tradesman with his deceased wife's sister, Arnold asks: "Who, that is not manacled and hoodwinked by his Hebraism, can believe that, as to love and marriage, our reason and the necessities of our humanity have their true, sufficient, and divine law expressed for them by the voice of an Oriental and polygamous nation like the Hebrews? Who, I say, will believe, when he really considers the matter, that where the feminine nature, the feminine ideal, and our relations to them, are brought into question, the delicate apprehensive genius of the Indo-European race is to find its last word on this question in the institutions of a Semitic people, whose wisest king had seven hundred wives and three hundred concubines?"

As it is impossible to reconcile this passage with the quotations given above ("of conduct the Bible is the great inspirer," etc.), this sudden extreme insistence on the Bible, including the Old Testament, as humanity's unique manual of conduct seems to be based less on reason than on an instinctive reversion to the idea of the Bible drilled into him in his early years. What caused this reversion? Partly, no doubt, a fear that the advance of the sceptics would sweep away the Bible altogether, a fear that would make him exaggerate the value of what he was defending. But deeper than this was the desire to establish an irresistible sanction for his own life-long adherence to conduct. At fifty a Puritan becomes uneasy. Has his view of conduct been based on a misunderstanding? Life as it recedes resumes the fascination it had for his youth. This mood of uneasiness seldom rises to the conscious mind. It suffices, however, to set him more continuously than in his earlier years to the task of justifying his morality.

"The object of religion is *conduct;* conduct is really, however one may overlay it with philosophical disquisitions, the simplest thing in the world as far as *understanding* is concerned; as regards *doing,* it is the hardest thing in the world."

Why, if the theory of conduct is so simple, the chosen people sanctioned polygamy, whereas the Indo-European shows an abstract preference for monogamy, is a question to which, with other questions of a like nature, Arnold was in too confused and excited a state to supply any answer.

"To one who knows what conduct is, it is a joy to be alive." Arnold recurs again and again to this theory that he is feeling extremely happy. "To righteousness belongs happiness. We believe that, indeed, 'salvation is of the Jews,' and that, for what concerns conduct or righteousness (that is, for what concerns three-fourths of human life), they and their documents can no more be neglected by whoever would make proficiency in it, than Greece can be neglected by anyone who would make proficiency in art, or Newton's discoveries by whoever would comprehend the world's physical laws. . . . Take a course of the Bible first, and then a course of Benjamin Franklin, Horace Greeley and Jeremy Bentham and Herbert Spencer; see which has most effect, which satisfies you most, which gives you most moral force."

The Hebrews with their revelation: "O ye that love the Eternal, see that ye hate the thing that is evil! To him that ordereth his conversation right, shall be shown the salvation of God"—the people to whom this revelation was given "deserve fully to be singled out as the Bible singles them. 'Behold, darkness doth cover the earth and gross darkness the nations; but the Eternal shall arise upon *thee*, and his glory shall shine upon thee.' . . . The word of this Eternal concerning Israel, as distinguished from every other nation of antiquity, is true, in spite of Israel's sacrifices and polygamy: 'You only have I known of all the families of the earth.' "

How did the Jews conceive of this Eternal, who, in the quotation just given, tells them that he has known them alone of all the families of the earth; adding, though Arnold does not quote this, "therefore I will punish you for all your iniquities"?

There seems to be a personal note in these words, but Arnold did not believe in a personal God, and having claimed for the Jews an instinct for righteousness derived from a unique connection with the Eternal, it was necessary to show that their idea of the Eternal was much the same as his.

The Archbishop of York, the Bishops of Winchester and Gloucester, and other contemporary theologians believed in "a personal First Cause, the moral and intelligent Governor of the universe." God, for Arnold, was "simply the stream of tendency by which all things seek to fulfil the law of their being." This he calls a scientific definition, but "the language of the Bible is literary, not scientific language; language *thrown out* at an object of consciousness not fully grasped, which

inspired emotion." The Jews therefore nowhere defined God as "a stream of tendency by which all things
seek to fulfil the law of their being," but they thought
of him, in a rough literary equivalent for this scientific
definition, as "a power which makes for righteousness."
or "a not ourselves which makes for righteousness."
To the idea of "a Great Personal First Cause, who
thinks and lives, the moral and intelligent Governor of
the Universe," the Bible, "rightly read, will," Arnold
states, "have nothing to say." Not then, a belief in a
God who loves and hates, who rewards and punishes,
but an intuition of a "not ourselves which makes for
righteousness" is the key-note of the Old Testament.

"This native, continuous and increasing pressure upon
Israel's spirit of the ideas of conduct and of its sanctions, we call his intuition of the Eternal that makes
for righteousness, the revelation to him of the religion
of this Eternal. Really, we do not know how else to
account for the evident fact of the pressure, than by
supposing that Israel had an intuitive faculty, a natural
bent for these ideas; that their truth was borne in upon
him, revealed to him. . . . Instead of remaining literature and philosophy, isolated voices of sublime poets
and reforming free-thinkers, these glorifications of
righteousness became Jewish religion, matters to be read
in the synagogue every Sabbath-day."

Before setting forth the passages in which Arnold
contradicts all the conclusions arrived at above, it will
be as well to summarize these conclusions:

1. No people ever felt so strongly as the people of the Old Testament that conduct is three fourths of our life.

2. The Jews of the Old Testament would have nothing to say to the view of God as a Great Personal First Cause.

3. The ideas of conduct and of its sanctions exercised a continuous and an increasing pressure upon the Jews of the Old Testament. These ideas were not confined to isolated poets and reformers; they were incorporated in the general life of the nation.

In rebuttal of these conclusions Arnold writes as follows: "It is evident that this revelation (of God as the Eternal that makes for Righteousness) lost, as time went on, its nearness and clearness; and that for the mass of the Hebrews their God came to be a mere magnified and non-natural man. And though prophets and righteous men, among the Hebrews, might preserve always the immediate and truer apprehension of their God as the Eternal who makes for Righteousness, they in vain tried to communicate this apprehension to the mass of their countrymen."

In this passage he contradicts conclusions No. 2 and No. 3. In another passage he contradicts both conclusion No. 2 (that the Jews did not think of God as a person), and the contradiction of conclusion No. 2 (that the Jews did think of God as a person, and were wrong so to think): "God, according to the Hebrews, is a father, because the power in and around us, which makes for righteousness, is indeed best described by the name of this authoritative yet tender and protecting relation."

Arnold has now left undemolished, though already much impaired, only conclusion No. 1: "No people ever felt so strongly as the people of the Old Testament that conduct is three-fourths of life."

With this he deals as soon as he passes from the Old Testament to the New. "Jesus Christ found Israel all astray, with an endless talk about God, the law, righteousness, the kingdom, everlasting life—and no hold upon any of them." The Jews "too much neglected the inward world of feelings and dispositions." The first need for Israel, therefore, "was to make religion cease to be mainly a national and social matter, and become mainly a personal matter."

In this last sentence Arnold marks the distinction between the Old Testament and the New, but without realizing that the New Testament would never have been carried through the world without the support of the Old; for the unique contribution of the people of the Old Testament to religion is not to be found, even by a more coherent and consistent seeker than Arnold, in their feeling for conduct or their intuition of the Eternal, but in the intense collective emotion generated in them by centuries of hostile attack, and carried on, through Saint Paul, into Christianity. Religion for the mass of man is a collective experience; the force of the emotion more than its contents is what wins them, and no nation has put such force into this form of religion as the Jews. Their literature is the expression of this collective emotion, in a degree unexampled in other literatures and fairly certain to remain unexampled; and therefore as long as the instinct to meet together to generate religious emotion survives, and there is no reason to believe it will ever be atrophied, readings from the Bible are unlikely ever to be superseded by readings from any other literature. The genius of the European poet or philosopher is individual and addresses itself to the individual; which explains why readings from Wordsworth or Plato to congregations of Rationalists miss the desired effect.

His treatment of the Old Testament exposes all Arnold's weak points, his desire to placate his father's shade, his tendency to personify a nation; and his treatment of conduct as though it were in no way related to the artistic and speculative elements in a man; all of which weaknesses derived from the continuous unresolved conflict between the repulsion he felt as an Englishman and a poet for the collective frenzies of a Semitic tribe and the habit enforced on him from his earliest years of placing this collective rampart between him and the perils to which the unsupported individual is exposed.

When he comes to Jesus, Arnold creates him, like Homer, in what he thought to be his own image, explaining as a misunderstanding of his reporters any

~~ DON MATTHEW ~~

(From a photograph taken by Sarony, in New York)

He created Jesus in his own Image

view expressed by Jesus with which he himself is not in agreement, and recurring again and again to the sweet reasonableness, and exquisite mild winning felicity of the passionate spirit who invoked the curse of Heaven on the unresponsive villages of his native district, and sought at last in death an escape from the conflict between his intuition of reality and his desire, condemned by this intuition itself, to communicate it to the world.

The reporters of Jesus, Arnold says, were "men liable to err, full of the turbid Jewish fancies about 'the grand consummation' which were then current." The more we understand this, he adds, "the less need we have to make Jesus a co-partner in their eschatology." Again, "who can read in the Gospels the comments preserved to us, both of disciples and of others, on what he said, and not feel that Jesus must have known, while he nevertheless persevered in saying them, how things like: 'Before Abraham was, I am,' or 'I will not leave you comfortless, I will come unto you,' would be misapprehended by those who heard them?"

Nor did miracles occur, or, if they did occur, they were not miracles. "When, however, our reader has accepted what we have to say about the untrustworthiness of miracles, and the looseness of the Gospel-record, his real work has still to begin. His work, in our view, is to learn to enjoy and turn to his benefit the Bible, as the word of the Eternal."

Arnold's aim in his theological writings was to persuade the Church of England to approximate its theology to his as the one sure means of securing itself against the infidel. Having, in the quotation just given, presented the word of the Eternal as inaccurate when not actually untrustworthy—not a reassuring formula for any Church to adopt—he goes on to use the authority of Jesus to wipe out at one stroke both the collective religion of the Old Testament and all forms of Christian institutionalism, including the Church of England; elsewhere described as "a great national society for the promotion of what is commonly called goodness."

"To take that chief stronghold of ecclesiasticism and sacerdotalism, the institution of the Eucharist. As Catholics present it, it makes the Church indispensable, with all her apparatus of an apostolical succession, an authorized priesthood, a power of absolution. Yet, as Jesus founded it, it is the most anti-ecclesiastical of institutions, pulverizing alike the historic churches in their beauty and the dissenting sects in their unloveliness;—it is the consecration of absolute individualism."

Here we may leave Arnold as theologian, thanking him, as we take our leave, for that well-turned phrase about the typical Nonconformist—"the precious discoveries of himself and his friends for expressing the inexpressible and defining the indefinable in peculiar terms of their own."

Arnold's habit of repeating certain key-words and phrases: sweetness and light, lucidity, lubricity, high seriousness, sweet reasonableness, criticism of life, conduct, disinterestedness, culture, Barbarians, Philistines, the object as in itself it really is, etc., has been attributed to a theory that only by incessant pressure can any new idea be urged into the head of an Englishman. A plausible theory; but I think this repetition was also due to an unconscious desire to strengthen his always uncertain hold on whatever idea had him in thrall at the moment.

Lubricity is a word which he used frequently in the last decade of his life. To refer to sensual indulgence as the worship of the Great Goddess Lubricity composed his nerves, as the reader will understand if he shrugs his shoulders and murmurs the phrase with a slight smile of distaste. The image evoked is ludicrous, not at all "troubling," as Arnold would say. By connecting the communal idea of worship with an emotion ill-suited to communal display, both the emotion and its expression are discredited. In his theological writings, however, he does not use the word, either because it had not yet fixed itself in his mind, or because it would have been out of tone in the context.

Lubricity, however, inhabited his mind during this period with, to borrow his own phrase about the Jews' intuition of the Eternal, "a native, continuous and increasing pressure." The two great Christian virtues were, he said, "charity and chastity, kindness and pureness." Charity he defines as "a kind of impersonal higher life, where the happiness of others counts with a man as essential to his own. He that loves his life does really turn out to lose it, and the commandment proves its own truth by experience. And the other great Christian virtue, pureness? Here the case is somewhat different. One hears doubts raised, nowadays, as to the natural truth of this virtue."

What did Arnold mean by pureness? He treats the subject so gingerly that it is difficult to extract any definite ideas from his scattered remarks. Tolstoi, who, in his final opinion, meant celibacy by pureness, would have regarded Dr. Arnold, the father of ten children, as patently impure. This cannot have been Matt's view.

Experience, he says, vaguely, must decide for or against pureness; and he quotes La Rochefoucauld: "There is no honest woman who is not sick of her trade," to which he opposes Ninon's confession, in her old age: "I pass for having enjoyed life, but if anyone had told me beforehand what my life was going to be I would have hanged myself." These two views, which are not mutually exclusive, do not get us much further; the only question they could raise in a young girl with an open mind on the subject being whether it was preferable to be wretched as an honest woman or as a Ninon de l'Enclos.

John Stuart Mill, quoted by Arnold, had recently stated that although he himself had in fact observed the Seventh Commandment "he did not consider the ordinances of society binding on a subject so entirely personal." Against Mill Arnold quotes Goethe: "In the notion of the sacredness of marriage, Christianity has got a culture-conquest of priceless value, although marriage is, properly speaking, unnatural;" and Arnold goes on: "Undoubtedly this notion of the sacredness of marriage came to Christianity from Israel. Such was Israel's genius for the ideas of moral order and of right, such was his intuition of the Eternal that makes for righteousness, that he felt without a shadow of doubt, and said with the most impressive solemnity, that Free Love was—to speak, again, like our modern philosophers—fatal to progress. 'He knows not that the dead are there, and that her guests are in the depths of hell.' "

Goethe was nearly sixty before he availed himself of the priceless culture-conquest of marriage, at which age he may have felt that the unnatural character he attributed to it would not press too heavily on him; but I shall come back in a minute to Goethe as a witness for pureness. The remainder of Arnold's argument is an excellent example of the lucid chaos in which he was accustomed to involve his ideas.

In order to confute Mill, who had said in effect that fidelity to one woman was a matter for each man to settle according to his own judgment, Arnold attributes the idea of monogamy to Israel, "whose wisest king had seven hundred wives and three hundred concubines," and quotes a warning maxim from the "Book of Proverbs" about prostitution as evidence that the Hebrews condemned Free Love, a phrase to which it is difficult to attach any meaning except that it excludes prostitution.

Finally, on behalf of whatever he is urging, Arnold quotes Goethe again: "May the idea of *pureness*, extending itself to the very morsel which I take into my mouth, grow ever clearer in me and clearer!" As an epicure, Goethe liked to heighten the pleasures of the senses by attaching the idea of pureness to the objects of these pleasures; and no doubt after a certain amount of auto-suggestion the chastity of a Frankfurter sausage moved him no less poignantly than its flavour, so that when he sat down to table his eyes would water as freely as his mouth; and what he felt about a sausage dissolving on his palate he would feel even more keenly about a girl dissolving in his arms. But of pureness, in its untransformed sense of abstinence, the sense, I am afraid, in which Arnold understood it, Goethe could never hear without an impatient gesture of disgust.

In the first six years of this period, from 1867 to 1877, Arnold's mother, one of his brothers, and three of his four sons died. Even apart from these losses, the ten years of his Crusade, the aim of which on the moral side was to persuade mankind that "to one who knows what conduct is it is a joy to be alive," appear from his letters to have been the most melancholy period of his life.

With five children and a comparatively small income his freedom was restricted in a way that irked him at times. In 1867 Arnold writes to his mother about the limitations imposed on his travels by his family, quoting:

> "O gin my sons were seven rats
> Runnin' o'er the castle wa',
> And I myself were a great grey cat,
> Fu' soon wad I worry them a'."

A letter to his brother, the Reverend E. P. Arnold, written in July, 1867, shows the temptations to travel which assailed him. "Sir James Shuttleworth wants me to come to his moor by Pennygant, in Yorkshire, for the beginning of the grouse shooting. . . . I shall perhaps be at liberty for a little run in Scotland with you, but it depends on the children, money, and many things. I have refused to go to the Grant Duffs' this year though they asked Flu and Tom with me."

The convention that man's wife must always be invited together with the husband was one by which Arnold seems to have been straitly bound. In the previous month he had taken Lady Airlie in to dinner at Balliol, and this letter to his brother concludes: "Lady Airlie asked me to Airlie, but she asked me by myself. I shall not go there either." From a letter to his mother, a few days later, we learn that Lady Airlie had made good the omission in her first letter. The joint invitation failed, however, of its effect. We learn, too, that Mrs. Arnold had been included in Sir James Shuttleworth's invitation to his grouse moor, a detail with which Arnold had forgotten to supply his brother.

Arnold's pleasure in shooting is rather surprising, and shows a bluntness of sensibility one does not find in, for example, Heine, in spite of the hardening effects of lubricity. It seems, however, that Arnold was a poor shot, another example, perhaps, of his divided impulses.

Against this flaw I must set a quotation from a letter to his mother, written about this time: "A teacher defending his school against a severe report of mine finished by saying that he had not a word against the Inspector, whom he would rather have than any other he had ever come in contact with, 'as he was always gentle and patient with the children.' "

At the beginning of 1868 Basil, who was not yet two, died. "And so," Arnold writes to "K.," "this loss comes to me just after my forty-fifth birthday, with so much other 'suffering in the flesh'—the departure of my youth, cares of many kinds, an almost painful anxiety about public matters—to remind us that *the time past of our life may suffice us*—words which have haunted me for the last year or two, and that we 'should no longer live the rest of our time in the flesh to the lusts of men, but to the will of God.' "

To his mother, a fortnight later, he speaks of "the thought of my little Basil, and resting by him in his quiet churchyard."

In February, Arnold and his family moved to Harrow, to Byron House, a house "with an old countrified Middlesex look."

The move to Harrow was probably made on Tom's account. Budge had been sent to Rugby, but Tom would be too delicate to leave home. In the previous year Arnold had written to his mother: "I met a Harrow master last night . . . owing to the sort of people who have gone there to send their sons to the school, there is absolutely nothing of that kind of slur on home-boarders, as they are called at Harrow, which falls on them elsewhere, and notably, as we know, at Rugby."

Forty years later, perhaps owing to the inferior quality of the people who had in the interval gone to Harrow to send their sons to the school, the social status of
a home-boarder at Harrow was analogous to that of a
Jew in a mediæval community. A friend of mine, when
I was at Harrow, once remarked to me: "I suppose you
realize it's very decent of me to be seen about with a
bloody home-bug like you." I have lost sight of him
since—but I digress.

Tom, after only one term at Harrow, died in the
November of this year. In a letter to his mother, a few
months later, Arnold writes: "It is a wonderfully clear,
bright day with a cold wind, so I went to a field on
the top of the hill, whence I can see the clumps of Bot-
ley and the misty line of the Thames, where Tommy
lies at the foot of them. I often go for this view on a
clear day"; and in another letter: "Before I left yesterday I saw dear Flu start for Laleham in a waggonette
with two greys, and Rover barking before them . . .
they were laden with plants, wreaths and flower-
crosses for the dear graves, and I was very glad Flu
should have an opportunity of making this expedition,
which had been long in her mind."

From this time on there are many references to
Rover, a retriever, and other dogs of the house, and to
Atossa, the Persian cat, in contemplating whom Arnold
would for the moment altogether forget that salvation
is of the Jews. "Atossa, or Toss, as we generally call
her, now lies stretched out on the floor by me, letting

the sunshine bathe all her deep, rich, tawny fur over her stomach; her ways are beautiful, as you will see when you have been with her a day."

"She (Atossa) curled herself up on the counter-pane by my side, and whenever I woke in the night she sat up instantly and looked at me; directly I lay down she curled herself up and slept again, and so she remained till I went down to breakfast the next morning."

Arnold, Mrs. Humphry Ward tells us, once went up to London from Harrow and brought Huxley back from the Athenæum, to examine the broken leg of Atossa, who, however, would have preferred the services of a qualified practitioner.

Budge, Arnold tells his mother in the spring of 1867, "looks well and seems very happy, but he brings a terrible character for idleness." Budge gradually settled down, and at the beginning of 1870 Arnold writes to his mother: "Budge's well-doing is a great pleasure to me, and I think he improves in all respects together." But within two years Budge, too, died. "I cannot write his name," Arnold says in a letter to his mother, "without stopping to look at it in stupefaction at his not being alive."

A Harrow master, the Rev. E. M. Young, wrote a copy of elegaics immediately after Budge's death, which Arnold acknowledges as follows: "Your verses give me very great pleasure, and I think they are, besides, very pleasing in themselves. Nothing will ever eradicate from me the feeling of the greater subtleness and adequateness, for a topic of this kind, of Latin Elegiacs than of any other descriptive verse."

In the following year, the Arnolds left Harrow for Cobham, in Surrey, which remained Arnold's home till his death.

During this decade he visited the Alps twice, but the Hebraic-paternal obsession of these years, lifted only at rare intervals, as in the contemplation of Atossa's sun-bathed stomach, follows him even to Switzerland. In 1869 he wrote to his mother: "I was saying the other day that if anyone were now to ask me whether I would sooner be going to Switzerland in August or going to Fox How, I could honestly say Fox How"; and two years later from Bel Alp he writes: "I myself feel more and more the deep satisfaction dear papa always felt in coming to Fox How even from the Continent; but I am one of the true likers of the Continent, as he, too, was." From Bel Alp as he looks across the great cleft of the Rhone Valley at the mountains above Zermatt, "the Matterhorn and the yet greater Mischabel," the name Mischabel sounds to him "as if the Hebrew race had been in these valleys."

If Amos, Micah, Jeremiah and the rest had returned to life, Arnold would have found himself awkwardly placed, for these prophets would not have understood their modern colleague's attitude towards the society he was trying to purify. "I think," Arnold writes to his mother in 1868, "Barbarian will stick; but as a very charming Barbarianess, Lady Portsmouth, expresses a great desire to make my acquaintance, I daresay the race will bear no malice"; and elsewhere: "I should think I heard the word Philistine used at least a hundred times during dinner"; and again: "Dizzy was in high force— He said to me across the table at dinner, à propos of something that was mentioned, 'Sweetness and light I call that, Mr. Arnold, eh?' "

Meredith nick-named Arnold "a dandy Isaiah," and he was also referred to as "a prophet of the kid-glove persuasion" and "an elegant Jeremiah"; but these are forced fruits, and I much prefer a little scene incidentally recorded by Arnold in a letter he wrote after a visit to a negro school during his American journey in 1883.

"I had to make a little speech to them," he writes, "and in return they sang, 'Dare to be a Daniel,' with negro energy."

XXXVI. THE LAST YEARS, 1877–1888

I WISH I could, here in this last entry, suddenly plunge the reader into an atmosphere altogether purged and renewed, reveal a vine-crowned Matt holding high revelry on the hills above his Surrey home, and allow a swift distant glimpse of George Russell pursuing Mrs. Humphry Ward through copse and glade.

Such a triumph for the Hellenizing tendency cannot be recorded. The fumes of the Hebrew marsh, even after he had got clear of it, lingered in Matt's brain to the end; but the virulent stage of the malady, during which he was unable to see the world as anything but a potential forcing-house of conduct, was definitely over by 1877.

In 1871, as he looked at the mountains above Zermatt, his fancy brooded on a possible incursion of Old Testament Jews into that region of pure beauty. At Bel Alp he remembered with a sensation of sympathy "the deep satisfaction dear papa always felt in coming to Fox How even from the Continent."

Nine years later, in September, 1880, he was in the Engadine, at Pontresina, in a mood which, especially when he describes the night flowing up from the valley, reminds one of his Cadmus and Harmonia, "in breathless quiet after all their ills." "It is no use denying," he wrote to his wife, "that the snow and the glaciers give a charm to the Alps which our mountains and Scotland can never possess"; and to Miss Arnold he writes: "It is worth coming abroad merely for this afternoon walk, high on the mountain side, with the great glacier below running up to the great snow-vested sweep of the Bernina and his fellow—all their upper parts sparkling in sunshine, but the deep black shadow steadily creeping up them."

In the previous year and again in the following year the most remarkable dawnist of the century, Nietzsche, was living within a few miles of Pontresina, at Sils-Maria. One wishes he had been there during Arnold's visit and that they had met. Both courteous and discreet, they would have enjoyed each other's society well enough for an hour, and have hoped, as they parted, for another meeting. But the mighty forces which at last wrecked Nietzsche's sanity would have been apprehended, though dimly, by Arnold, and he would not have felt any real wish to see Nietzsche again.

Arnold and Nietzsche have both described a similar scene in the Engadine.

"What you would greatly like," Arnold writes to his wife, "is the sight of the Bergamesque herdsmen, who have been feeding their herds on the pastures here for the summer, collecting them to drive them back to Italy. The men are picturesque objects, tall, swarthy Italians, with their civilized speech instead of the rough guttural German. And their cattle are too lovely. I could have stayed till night yesterday to see a herd driven through the swollen torrent of the Roseg, which lay between their Alp and the road to Italy. In one place they had to swim, poor things, but it was beautiful to see how well they managed, greatly as they disliked it."

Nietzsche writes: "Before me a flock moved, now scattering, now closing up its ranks; some cows, grouped afar-off, below a forest of pines, stood out in relief under the evening light; others, nearer, more sombre; and everything calm in the peace of the approaching twilight. My watch registered half-past five. The monarch of the herd was walking in the foam-white brook; he stepped out slowly, now stemming the fierce tide, now giving way to it: no doubt he found a kind of ferocious delight in so doing. Two human beings, of Bergamesque origin, were the shepherds of this flock. . . ."

In March, 1881, Arnold wrote to a French friend, Monsieur Fontanès: "Whoever treats religion, religious discussions, questions of churches and sects, as absorbing, is not in vital sympathy with the movements of men's minds at present." There was showing itself in the middle class, he said, a wonderful relaxation of the old strictness as to theatres, dancing, and such things; and of this relaxation he approved. "The awakening demand for beauty, a demand so little made in this country for the last century and more, is another sign of the revolution. . . . Man feels himself to be a more various and richly endowed animal than the old religious theory of human life allowed, and he is endeavouring to give satisfaction to the long-suppressed and still imperfectly-understood instincts of this varied nature."

Here we have the Prodigal Son, a Jewish gaberdine hanging in rags on his wasted frame, returning to his Indo-European father. But he was nearly sixty now, and the return was too late.

Among the subjects he treated during his last ten or eleven years in "Mixed Essays" and the second series of "Essays in Criticism," were Goethe and George Sand, Milton, Wordsworth, Byron, Gray, Burns, Keats, Tolstoi, and Shelley. In his critical work, as in his poetry, the merit of his writing is in inverse proportion to the greatness of the subject. As literature, the essays on the de Guérins are above comparison with his "Lectures on Homer," or even with his essay on Heine; and in these later studies he succeeds better with Gray, in whose mournful life and scanty production he saw himself in an eighteenth-century setting, than with any of the others, except George Sand, the only writer in this list who can possibly be ranked below Gray. She, as even the least scrupulous of my readers must remember, was part of Arnold's youth, and on her, and especially on the country of her novels, Arnold writes his most natural and most deeply felt prose.

But apart from his being better suited with comparatively slight subjects, his return to his own sphere was too late, because the intervening years had withered his spontaneous delight in poetry. After "Balder Dead" and "Merope," he had decided that the age he lived in was adverse to the creative faculty, and that he must divert his powers to criticism. Henceforth criticism took on an ever-increasing importance in his eyes. Theoretically he continued to rank the creative faculty higher, but in particular instances he found, whenever at all possible, reasons for ranking a man's critical above his creative work, or the criticism of one man above the creation of another.

"The great men of culture," he wrote in "Culture and Anarchy," "are those who have had a passion for diffusing, for making prevail, for carrying from one society to the other, the best knowledge, the best ideas of their time. . . . Such were Lessing and Herder in Germany. . . . Generations will pass, and literary monuments will accumulate, and works far more perfect than the works of Lessing and Herder will be produced in Germany; and yet the names of these two men will fill a German with a reverence and enthusiasm such as the names of the most gifted masters will hardly awaken."

Of these gifted German masters, the greatest is Goethe. Arnold would perhaps not have said bluntly that Lessing and Herder awaken more enthusiasm than Goethe; but in "A French Critic on Goethe," he manages to suggest that Goethe himself is more important as critic than as creator. Coaxing his reader past all Goethe's creative work, except the lyrics and the first part of *Faust*, he then, without any explanation, turns his back on *Faust* and the lyrics, and concludes: "It is not principally in his published works, it is in the immense Goethe-literature of letter, journal, and conversation, in the volumes of Riemer, Falk, Eckermann, the Chancellor von Müller, in the letters to Merck and Madame van Stein and many others, in the correspondence with Schiller, the correspondence with Zelter, that the elements for an impression of the truly great, the truly significant Goethe are to be found."

This tendency to prefer criticism to creation, to find the sign-posts in a landscape more attractive and significant than the scenery, derived ultimately from the emotional repression which had dried up his own poetry. Passion and ecstasy, in poetry, had come to be distasteful to him, not only because these qualities could not find expression in the critical work to which he had given his best years, but also because he had missed or avoided them in life itself.

In the "Study of Poetry," which he contributed in 1880 as an introduction to Mr. T. H. Ward's "English Poets," he defined poetry as "a criticism of life," adding, as a precaution against attack, "under the conditions fixed for such a criticism by the laws of poetic truth and poetic beauty." This attempt to turn poetry itself into criticism he developed still further in his essay on Wordsworth. "The noble and profound application of ideas to life is the most essential part of poetic greatness . . . under the conditions immutably fixed by the laws of poetic beauty and poetic truth," and in support of this position he quoted Voltaire: "No nation has treated in poetry moral ideas with more energy and depth than the English nation." This remark of Voltaire's, which occurs in his "Age of Louis XIVth," is illustrated with two examples, Dryden and Pope. Dryden and Pope, however, did not fit into Arnold's argument. Their verse, he had said in "The Study of Poetry," was "admirable for the purposes of an age of prose and reason." He therefore explains that Voltaire did not mean by treating moral ideas "the composing moral and didactic poems. He means the application of these ideas under the conditions fixed for us by the laws of poetic beauty and poetic truth."

What the conditions fixed for us by the laws of poetic beauty and poetic truth are, Voltaire does not tell us in his "Age of Louis XIVth," nor, I believe, elsewhere. Nor does Arnold attempt in any way to elucidate this definition, which he keeps on repeating as if in the hope that enough repetitions will suddenly make it clear, if not to himself at least to his readers.

No refutations will shake a man who is developing an argument in which he does not really believe; but he is pulled up short when someone agrees, or seems to agree, with him. This theory of Arnold's that ideas are pegs for a poet to hang his poems on, Arnold regarded with distaste when he found it, or thought he found it, in Leslie Stephen's essay on Wordsworth, an essay at all points superior to Arnold's.

"The fervent Wordsworthian," Arnold writes, "will add, as Leslie Stephen adds, that Wordsworth's poetry is precious because his philosophy is sound; that his 'ethical system is as distinctive and capable of exposition as Bishop Butler's'; that his poetry is informed by ideas which 'fall spontaneously into a scientific system of thought.' But we must learn to be on our guard against the Wordsworthians, if we want to secure for Wordsworth his due rank as a poet. The Wordsworthians are apt to praise him for the wrong things, and to lay far too much stress upon what they call his philosophy. His poetry is the reality, his philosophy—so far, at least, as it may put on the form and habit of 'a scientific system' of thought, and the more that it puts them on—is the illusion. Perhaps we shall one day learn to make this proposition general, and to say: Poetry is the reality, philosophy the illusion."

Not having Stephen's essay by me, I do not know if Arnold is quoting him in the phrase, which is not in Stephen's usual style, "Wordsworth's poetry is precious because his philosophy is sound," but the words actually given from Stephen imply the reverse conclusion, that Wordsworth's philosophy is sound because his poetry is precious; a vital distinction never consciously grasped by Arnold, whose theory that criticism precedes creation I have already discussed.

When Arnold thought he found his own view expressed by Stephen, the shock sent him too far in the opposite direction, and having first made the cart of philosophy draw the horse of poetry, he now places the horse where he should have been from the first, and then ignores the cart as an illusion.

The little that is of value in Arnold's essay on Wordsworth is written under the influence of this shock. "Wordsworth's poetry, when he is at his best, is inevitable, as inevitable as nature herself. . . . Nature herself seems to take the pen out of his hand, and to write for him with her own bare, sheer, penetrating power." But, having gone so far, his shrinking from emotion prevents him from giving any example of Wordsworth at the height of his unique power. "The right sort of verse to choose from Wordsworth, if we are to seize his true and most characteristic form of expression, is a line like this from 'Michael':

> 'And never lifted up a single stone.' "

This emotional petrifaction shows itself again and again throughout these essays. He prefers Gray's "Odes" to his "Elegy in a Country Churchyard," and Gray would have no doubt returned the compliment by ranking "Sohrab and Rustum" above "The Forsaken Merman." "Gray himself, however, maintained that the 'Elegy' was not his best work in poetry, and he was right." Shelley he worries whenever a chance shows itself. "Shelley praises Byron too unreservedly, but he sincerely felt, and he was right in feeling, that Byron was a greater poetical power than himself. Nay, I doubt whether his (Shelley's) delightful 'Essays and Letters,' which deserve to be far more read than they are now, will not resist the wear and tear of time better, and finally come to stand higher than his poetry"; and, in his survey of Burns, "a beast with splendid gleams" as he calls him in a letter written at this time, Arnold seeks Burns' assistance to sterilize both Shelley and Burns himself at the height of his imaginative passion.

"We all of us have a leaning towards the pathetic,

and may be inclined perhaps to prize Burns most for
his touches of piercing, sometimes almost intolerable,
pathos, for verse like:

> 'We twa hae paidl't i' the burn,
> From mornin' sun till dine;
> But seas between us braid hae roared
> Sin aul lang syne. . . .'

where he is as lovely as he is sound. But perhaps it is
by the perfection of soundness of his lighter and archer
masterpieces that he is poetically most wholesome for
us. For the votary misled by a personal estimate of
Shelley no contact can be wholesomer than the contact
with Burns at his archest and soundest. Side by side with
the:

> 'On the brink of the night and the morning
> My coursers are wont to respire,
> But the earth has just whispered a warning
> That their flight must be swifter than fire. . . .'

of 'Prometheus Unbound,' how salutary, how very
salutary, to place this from 'Tam Glen':

> 'My Minnie does constantly deave me
> And bids me beware o' young men;
> They flatter, she says, to deceive me;
> But wha can think sae o' Tam Glen?' "

A jet of enthusiasm spurts out now and then, as in
the "Essay on Keats" where Arnold praises "Keats'
rounded perfection and felicity of loveliness." This

relaxation of his usual attitude he perhaps felt he had earned by his remarks on a letter written by Keats to Fanny Brawne, when Keats was already advanced in his fatal illness, too poor, even if he had been in good health, to marry, and tortured without respite by the contrast between his own passion and Fanny Brawne's amiable affection.

"Keats' love-letter is the letter of a surgeon's apprentice. It has in its relaxed self-abandonment something underbred and ignoble, as of a youth ill brought up. . . . The sensuous man speaks in it, and the sensuous man of a badly bred and badly trained sort."

By this date, as this passage shows, Arnold's nerves were in disorder on all questions connected with sex. Burns, we have seen, was a beast with splendid gleams. Keats, we now learn, was a bounder. Goethe, as pre-eminently a critic and also as a champion of marriage, is treated more carefully and not directly. On the subject of Goethe's connection with Christiana Vulpius, Arnold quotes his French critic, Scherer, for whose opinions he had great respect and whose son had been christened after Dr. Arnold. "A degrading connection," Scherer calls it, "with a girl of no education, whom Goethe established in his house to the great embarrassment of all his friends, whom he either could not or would not marry until eighteen years later, and who punished him as he deserved by taking to drink."

Finally, Shelley, in Arnold's last piece of writing, a review of Professor Dowden's Life of Shelley, is dealt with almost exclusively in his sexual relations. "After

reading his (Dowden's) book, one feels sickened for
ever of the subject of irregular relations; . . . What a
set! What a world! . . . Godwin's house of sordid
horror, and Godwin preaching and holding the hat, and
the green-spectacled Mrs. Godwin, and Hogg the faithful friend, and Hunt the Horace of this precious world,
and, to go up higher, Sir Timothy Shelley, a great country gentleman, feeling himself safe while 'the exalted
mind of the Duke of Norfolk (the drinking Duke) protects me with the world,' and Lord Byron with his deep
grain of coarseness and commonness; his affectation, his
brutal selfishness—what a set! The history carries us
to Oxford, and I think of the clerical and respectable
Oxford of those old times, the Oxford of Copleston,
and the Kebles, and Hawkins. . . . I am not only
thinking of morals, and the house of Godwin; I am
thinking also of tone, bearing, dignity. I appeal to
Cardinal Newman, if perchance he does me the honour
to read these words, is it possible to imagine Copleston
or Hawkins declaring himself safe 'while the exalted
mind of the Duke of Norfolk protects me with the
world'?"

We do not know how Copleston or Hawkins figured
in the imagination of Cardinal Newman, but nowadays
I suppose there cannot be a score of persons with any
material about Copleston or Hawkins for their imagination to work on; whereas Shelley and Byron still live
in our minds; and Shelley, "a beautiful and ineffectual
angel" in Arnold's phrase, with increasing power and
beauty. This is a fact of more significance than the

squalid persons or circumstances that formed part of Shelley's experience. Of these persons and circumstances we cannot know too much, but it is necessary to see them in perspective. Professor Dowden of course made no attempt to see anything connected with Shelley in perspective. Had he discovered Shelley to be a cannibal with an avowed preference for the flesh of new-born infants, he would have smiled tenderly over Shelley's love of children. But Professor Dowden could have been dealt with without disentombing Copleston and Hawkins; though it would be disingenuous of me to affect dismay at this error of Arnold's, for no more appropriate last appearance of the poet of "The Forsaken Merman" could be demanded by the argument of this book than Arnold peering uneasily at Shelley from behind the skirts of Cardinal Newman.

To the general rule that in his last two years Arnold shrank from poetry, there are two exceptions, both more apparent than real, his praise of Byron and of Milton. At Winchester he had won a prize for declaiming Byron's "Marino Faliero." Byron must have been, in his boyhood and youth, his chief refuge from Dr. Arnold; and his essay on Byron, in which he ranks Byron with Wordsworth above all other English poets of the nineteenth century, should therefore not be censured as criticism but approved as an act of filial impiety.

With Milton, Arnold was reconciled to the poetry by the pureness of the poet. "Milton's power of style has for its great character *elevation;* and Milton's elevation clearly comes, in the main, from a moral quality in him

—his pureness. . . . He is our great artist in style, our one first-rate master in the grand style."

But Arnold adds: "Excuse them how one will, Milton's asperity and acerbity, his want of sweetness of temper, of the Shakespearean largeness and indulgence, are undeniable."

It did not occur to him that asperity and acerbity will show themselves in a man's style as well as pureness. He speaks of Milton's "perfect sureness of hands in his style," and certainly Milton's continuous command of rhythm is unequalled, but the character of the man, his conceit, and pomposity, come out even in his most impersonal passages:

"Meanwhile the tepid caves, and fens, and shores,
  Their brood as numerous hatch from the egg, that soon,
  Bursting with kindly rupture, forth disclosed
  Their callow young; but feathered soon and fledge,
  They summed their pens, and soaring the air sublime,
  With clang despised the ground. . . ."

or

"Up stood the corny reed
  Embattled in her field: add the humble shrub
  And bush with frizzled hair implicit."

How did Arnold manage to include passages like this in his formula of "elevation," or how did he reconcile the contrast between Milton's hard selfish temper and Shakespeare's "largeness and indulgence" with his general views of pureness? Yet, if he were alive, I should shrink from posing him with such, as far as I can see, unanswerable problems. A man's views are simply his apology for himself, and an apology personally tendered cannot very well be rejected.

"Wronsky's gifts and graces hardly qualify him, one might think, to be the object of so instantaneous and mighty a passion on the part of a woman like Anna, but let us allow that one of the male sex scarcely does justice, perhaps, to the powerful and handsome guardsman and his attractions."

In his essay on Tolstoi, theoretically so ruthless a moralist, Arnold's Hellenizing tendency bestirs itself in self-defence. In his analysis of Anna Karenina, he shows a really charming tenderness and concern for Anna, and a creditable annoyance with Wronsky for capturing her so quickly and so completely. "We see the gray eyes with their long eye-lashes, the graceful carriage, the gentle and caressing smile on the fresh lips, the vivacity restrained but waiting to break through, the fulness of life, the softness and strength joined, the harmony, the bloom, the charm"; and then of Anna's suicide, "It is over—the graceful head is untouched, but all the rest is a crushed, formless heap. Poor Anna!"

Still, salvation continues to be of the Jews, and Arnold has to congratulate Tolstoi on not putting in any touches at the dictation of the Goddess Lubricity. "Nothing is of a nature to trouble the senses, or to please those who wish their senses troubled." Poor Matt!

The essay ends, however, on the Hellenizing note.

"Count Tolstoi has perhaps not done well in abandoning the work of the poet and artist, and might with advantage return to it"; and the essay written in the same year, 1887, on Amiel, ends with the same moral, that a man with literary gifts should not employ them on theology or metaphysics.

In this last decade, Arnold wrote four poems, all elegies; two on dogs, Geist and Kaiser, one on a canary, Matthias, and one on a dean, Stanley.

Of "Westminster Abbey," the elegy on Stanley, Arnold said in a letter: "Many will think, no doubt, as they did about 'Thyrsis' at first, that there should have been more of direct personal effusion as to the departed and to my feelings towards him. However, one can only do these things in one's own way."

The poem, a very fine study in the manner of Milton's "Nativity Ode," contains of real feeling perhaps only three lines:

> Yet would I not disturb thee from thy tomb,
>   Thus sleeping in thine Abbey's friendly shade,
>   And the rough waves of life for ever laid!

and the feeling here is not connected with Stanley. For direct personal effusion on the part of Arnold, especially in these later years, we must not look outside his family, and his dogs.

There is, as frontispiece to Matthew Arnold's Birthday Book, published in 1883, a photograph of Arnold with the dachshund Max on his lap. The mouth is

~ MATTHEW AND MAX ~

The Frontispiece to "Matthew Arnold's Birthday Book,"
1883

querulous and discontented, but otherwise his expression, as he looks down at Max, is gentle and exceedingly sad. No other likeness I have seen corresponds so nearly with the impression his later writings make on me; most certainly not the portrait in the National Gallery by Watts, of Arnold as scholar, poet, and gentleman.

Max and Kaiser were the successors to Geist, who died in 1880, and whom Arnold commemorated in "Geist's Grave."

> "And so there rise these lines of verse
>   On lips that rarely form them now;
> While to each other we rehearse:
> Such ways, such arts, such looks hadst thou!
>
> "We stroke thy broad brown paws again,
> We bid thee to thy vacant chair,
> We greet thee by the window-pane,
> We hear thy scuffle on the stir.
>
> "We see the flaps of thy large ears
>   Quick raised to ask which way we go;
> Crossing the frozen lake, appears
> Thy small black figure on the snow."

"My darling boy," Arnold wrote to his son in Australia about these verses, "I hoped to have sent you to-day my lines about your dear, dear little boy, but I have not yet been able to get a correct copy from the printer. . . . I like to think of all the newspapers having his dear little name in them when the Xmas number of the *Fortnightly* is advertised, and I hope people will like the lines, and that will lead to his being more mentioned and talked about, which seems to be a sort of continuation of him in life, dear little fellow, though it is but a hollow and shadowy one. . . . I am always, my darling boy, your most loving Papa."

Some years later, in 1885, he writes to his elder daughter, who was married to an American, and lived in New York: "Nearly every day, Miss Lu, I go home to luncheon and take the dear man (Max) his round in Hyde Park afterwards; he quite expects it, and is the best of boys. . . . Your letters are delightful, my child; I always cry when they are read to me; but it is a happy cry."

In the following year, 1886, when he was on the Continent for the last time, on an official visit to the schools of Switzerland and Bavaria, he writes to his wife, who had sent him news of the death of Lola, the pony.

"You tell it beautifully, just all that I should naturally want to know; and all that you have done is exactly right, and as I could wish. Perhaps we might have kept a *mèche* of her hair where it used to come over her forehead. . . . There was something in her character which I particularly liked and admired, and I shall never forget her, dear little thing! The tears come into my eyes as I write."

On the same journey he wrote to his daughter, Eleanor, from Nuremberg: "Oh, Miss Nelly, what do you think I saw in one of the open places—the darling himself, the same colour, the same sex, the same age, the same size, the same slow and melancholy way; his eyes were yellower than Max's, that was the only difference. The extraordinary and more than natural crook of one foreleg was the same. He looked at me wistfully, as if to say:: 'I know you, but we must not speak here.' "

Later Arnold met Max's double once more: "I had again that weird look from him, as if to say we were in a dream, and must dream on."

Nor was it merely comfort for his heart the dogs gave him in these last years. They were of practical service, too. "The only drawback to the Cobham visits," Mrs. Humphry Ward writes, "were the 'dear, dear boys'—*i. e.*, the dachshunds, Max and Geist, who, however adorable in themselves, had no taste for visitors and no intention of letting such intruding creatures interfere with their possession of their master; one would go down to Cobham, eager to talk to 'Uncle Matt' about a book or an article—covetous at any rate of *some* talk with him undisturbed. And it would all end in a breathless chase after Max, through field after field where the little wretch was harrying either sheep or cows, with the dear poet, hoarse with shouting, at his heels. The dogs were always *in the party*, talked to, caressed, or scolded exactly like spoilt children; and the cat of the house was almost equally dear."

During this period Arnold went to America twice, once in 1886 to visit his daughter, and three years earlier on a lecturing tour, the fruit of which was his "Discourses in America," the book, of all his prose, he most wished to be remembered by.

There are three Discourses, on "Numbers," on "Literature and Science," and on "Emerson."

The middle discourse, on "Literature and Science," is an argument of literature against science as the chief instrument in education, literature being understood to include law, military, history, and the results of scientific study, but not their processes.

Although he presents himself, in accordance with his customary formula, as "a being of dim faculties and bounded knowledge," the discourse is otherwise free from affectation and is well argued. As a writer, Arnold was chastened, while composing these lectures, by the knowledge that he would have his audience in the body before him, a knowledge that with the rhetorical type has unfortunately the reverse of a chastening effect.

In the first of the Discourses, "Numbers," Arnold suggests to his audience his reasons for looking at America with a sanguine eye from the dawnist standpoint. Isaiah had hoped for the redemption of Israel, and had placed his hopes in the remnant of righteous men still to be found among the Jews.

"But," Arnold says, "he puts the leader's coming, and he put the success of the leader's and the remnant's work far too soon; and his conception in this respect is fantastic. . . . Immanuel and the remnant could not come to reign under the conditions there and then offered to them; the thing was impossible.

diagnosed by his doctor as indigestion, not heart. Early in '87 he wrote to Mrs. Coates: "The tendency to pain in the chest diminished as soon as I went on board ship to return home; and now, in the friendly air of this dear, stupid old country, has almost entirely disappeared."

A few years earlier he had written to John Morley: "I have no wish to execute the Dance of Death in an elementary school." Morley and Arnold were friends, and it may have been as the unintended result of this remark that Gladstone in the following year conferred a pension of £250 on Arnold "as a public recognition of service to the poetry and literature of England." Arnold was reluctant to accept this pension, but finally yielded, to the disgust of *The Echo*, a Liberal and Nonconformist paper, which spoke of him as "a very Bonaparte for rapacity."

With this pension, and what his writings, and later his lectures, brought him, he was in a position to retire, though his retirement did not actually take place till the end of 1886.

His last letters are full of trees and flowers. Mrs. Arnold visited her daughter in America in the spring of '86, and Arnold sent her news of the flowers in their Cobham garden: "Poor Gina's camellia has been very handsome indeed; the dentarias, too, are beautiful, and the great azalea is splendid. The scented rhododendron has nine blows on it, and will be out in a day or two. . . . As you say, 'we are too old for these separations,' and I cannot bear them." Two months later, from

America, Arnold wrote to his wife, in Cobham, "And the fringe-tree and the wigged sumach!—this latter growing with a strength of shoot and an exuberance of wig which one never sees in England."

One of his last letters was to "K.," the favourite sister of his earlier years. "We drove to Chequers . . . hills crowned with beechwoods, with combes full of box, and pure green spaces here and there among the box." But the last letter of all does not speak of flowers. "I found Lady Charles Beresford enthralled by 'Robert Elsmere,' tell Mary [1]. . . . George Russell was here a day or two ago; he was staying at Aston Clinton with Gladstone, and says it is all true about his interest in the book; he talked of it incessantly."

Five days later, on April 15th, 1888, Arnold died suddenly of heart failure. He had gone to Liverpool with his wife, to meet their elder daughter, but his death occurred before she reached England. He was sixty-five years old, and a few months.

There is a passage in one of these later letters which unites the most essential elements of a life that was more lonely even than most lives, easily discouraged by its surroundings and the crudeness of common humanity, but solaced every now and then by brief glimpses of beauty. "I had a cold journey to Wigan, and on the platform there it was windy and dismal. They told me at the booking-office there was no chance of a berth in a sleeping-car, but when the train came up the guard of the Perth carriage told me he had one. He threw open

---

[1] Mrs. Humphry Ward, the author of "Robert Elsmere."

a door, and revealed a pursy man on his back in bed, close to whom I should have had to lie. I said, no thank you, and tumbled into an empty first-class carriage, where I soon made myself a nest.

"At Stirling I pulled up the blinds just in time to see the long line of the Grampians, clothed half-way down with snow, shining in the morning light like the line of the Alps seen from Turin."

Thonon, Lake of Geneva.